The Mindful Art of Space Making

How to Declutter When You're Overwhelmed

by April Scott Tandy

Flume Canyon Publishing
www.flumecanyonpublishing.com

Copyright © 2024 by April Scott Tandy

All rights reserved.

No portion of this book may be reproduced in any form without written permission from the publisher or author, except as permitted by U.S. copyright law.

This publication is designed to provide accurate and authoritative information in regard to the subject matter covered. It is sold with the understanding that neither the author nor the publisher is engaged in rendering legal, investment, accounting or other professional services. While the publisher and author have used their best efforts in preparing this book, they make no representations or warranties with respect to the accuracy or completeness of the contents of this book and specifically disclaim any implied warranties of merchantability or fitness for a particular purpose. No warranty may be created or extended by sales representatives or written sales materials. The advice and strategies contained herein may not be suitable for your situation. You should consult with a professional when appropriate. Neither the publisher nor the author shall be liable for any loss of profit or any other commercial damages, including but not limited to special, incidental, consequential, personal, or other damages.

First edition, 2024

Cover design by Kam Bains

Developmental editing by Jackson Tandy

Published by Flume Canyon Publishing
www.flumecanyonpublishing.com

Space Maker Method
www.spacemakermethod.com

For my family

Contents

Prologue	VI
What is Space Making?	XIV

Stage 1: The Before

Introduction to Stage 1: The Before	2
1. Take the Pressure Off by Setting Realistic Expectations	3
2. Examine Your Clutter by Performing a Walk Through	14
3. Guarantee Success with Motivation & Accountability	23

Stage 2: The During

Introduction to Stage 2: The During	34
4. Simplify the Starting Process: Start Here!	36
5. Decluttering Made Simple: Sort Your Stuff Into the Easy Eight	50
6. Focus Your Attention to Build Unstoppable Momentum	71

7. Mindfully Process Your Belongings for the Benefit of Yourself & Others ... 79

8. How to Navigate Difficult Emotions & Keep Moving Forward ... 90

9. How to Know When You've Decluttered Enough ... 95

Stage 3: The After

Introduction to Stage 3: The After ... 104

10. Make Life Easier & More Enjoyable: Organize Like a Space Maker ... 106

11. Shop Your Own Home: Design Like a Space Maker ... 119

12. Routine Maintenance & Behavioral Change: The Responsibility is Yours ... 129

Stay Connected ... 140

Acknowledgements ... 141

Glossary of Terms ... 144

Prologue

Where did "Space Making" come from?

In 2020, I quit my day job to pursue my passion for helping people improve their homes. I started the YouTube channel that is now called "Space Maker Method" and began featuring many of my client projects on the channel.

Looking back now, I am extremely grateful for everyone who allowed me to work in their homes. Starting out, I had my own ideas of how I could help people in their homes, but all those years "in the trenches" taught me what really works and what doesn't. The ideas in this book are not just my opinions; they are hard-earned lessons from years of problem-solving with real people in real homes.

So the Space Maker method has been evolving ever since 2020, but the phrase "Space Maker" was not something I used in the beginning. It's something that happened organically.

One day I was filming a video and I had been decluttering all day. During this particular video there came a moment when I finished sorting a huge pile of stuff. I stood back to admire my work. Then

I suddenly turned to the camera, flexed my muscles, and yelled in my best Arnold Schwarzenegger voice,

"I am the Space Maker!"

I didn't really know what I was saying. I was exhausted but also proud of the space I'd created as a result of my hard work.

To my surprise, my viewers thought it was funny and the term Space Maker stuck. They started joking about how they were Space Makers too, or how they were "embodying the spirit of the Space Maker." They said it helped them gain the courage to face challenging tasks, like putting on a Superman cape. And this brings me to a very important point.

The best part of my work is not donating old clothes or organizing kitchen cabinets. The best part of my work is empowering people to tackle difficult tasks they've been avoiding. That's the goal of this book. I'm going to teach you how to fish instead of giving you one of my fish (did I get that expression right?).

When you become a Space Maker, you start to become something that you weren't before. Notice how my clients can't help but hint at the change in themselves as they rave about the change in their homes.

> *"I always avoided coming home, but now I can't wait to get here! My house is better than a hotel!"*

"Your method saved my marriage. My husband and I no longer fight over our messy space."

"I'm no longer embarrassed to invite guests over. I'm proud to show off my home."

"There's always been some things I wanted to get rid of, but was mentally incapable of doing so, and your method helped guide me to do it on my own time, at my own pace."

"Your process has made me feel like it's okay to own things you love. And it's okay to keep something you don't use and revisit later when you're ready."

"The last thing we want to do is start sorting through our lifetime of crap. But, thanks to your method, I've realized this is something that not only I can do, but I have to do."

"I have more space for my art projects and I've finished so many projects since!"

Hopefully by now you've realized that this book is not a random list of tips and tricks. It's a comprehensive guide to a transformative journey that anyone can undertake if they are brave enough to begin.

Who is This Book For?

This book is for people who are overwhelmed with their home and want to take action. People who dream of *something better* than a house full of clutter.

I've helped all kinds of people transform their chaotic spaces. I've worked with singles, couples, and families. I've worked in big homes and tiny apartments, in countries all over the world, but it's not really accurate to say that I help *everyone,* because I tend to help a certain kind of person. You might even say I have a "type."

My clients all have these four traits in common.

#1 They have lots of stuff.

I'm not talking about a few extra sweaters. I'm talking about mountains of clothes. Garages full of family heirlooms. Overflowing closets, rooms you can't walk through, blocked doors, exploding drawers, doom piles galore. At the very least, they have more than they would like.

#2 They want to live with less.

The clutter is affecting their life in a negative way. My clients like their stuff, but admittedly they have too much. They will never be—nor do they want to be—an extreme minimalist with two spoons and a t-shirt, but something needs to give. They could make better use of their space if only they could reduce the clutter.

#3 They want to declutter mindfully.

A lot of their stuff is useful or has sentimental value. Items were gifted or passed down to them, or they represent cherished memories. No way are my clients just going to throw it all away! They would rather use their stuff. And if they can't use it, they'd rather donate, recycle, re-gift, or repurpose it. At the very least they'd like to sell some items to recoup the cost.

#4 They are overwhelmed.

They don't know where to start. The project is too big, the process too emotional. When they do work up the courage to start, they inevitably get overwhelmed during the **Messy Middle** and quit. The task before them seems impossible.

A good portion of my clients have completely given up hope. They've resigned themselves to the sad reality that things will never get better.

If you identify with my clients, this book can help you.

Even if you have minimal clutter, this book will help you make more mindful decisions about the possessions you keep and how you keep them. Not only will you learn to create an orderly home filled only with the things you love, you'll also learn how to maintain that peaceful feeling for ever after.

How Will This Book Help Me?

The problem of "how to declutter" is a serious one, and many of my clients have tried other methods that didn't work for them.

For example, some methods say you should begin by decluttering all of your clothes. Sounds simple, right? But for many of my clients the clothing category is a huge task, and starting there is a great way to get discouraged immediately. Other methods encourage you to declutter all of your belongings in a single pass, which for my clients is completely unrealistic. They need **Multiple Passes**.

Minimalism is another popular solution to the problem of having too much stuff, but most minimalist advice doesn't resonate with my clients at all. When they hear things like "if you haven't worn it in 6 months, throw it out," or "if it costs less than $20, just throw it away and re-buy it later," they are likely to turn and run. Or scoff. Or laugh.

But feeling overwhelmed by your clutter is no laughing matter. It's a complex problem, mentally, physically, and emotionally. A stranger can't fix it for you. It can't be fixed overnight, and it can't be fixed with brute force. It needs to be navigated *mindfully*.

So let me introduce you to *The Mindful Art of Space Making*. And let me tell you exactly why this book—and the method it outlines—are going to help you.

The Space Maker Method:

- encourages you to go at your own pace, making careful decisions that you won't regret later.

- focuses on starting small with **Quick Wins** to build your confidence.

- helps you make difficult decisions about emotional and sentimental items.

- doesn't focus on the number of items you own as long as you are being intentional about your choices.

- guides you through a process with 3 distinct stages (1-**Before**, 2-**During**, 3-**After**) so that you never feel lost or overwhelmed.

Most importantly, the goal of this book is to motivate and empower you. Tips and tricks are fine, but none of it matters if you're lacking confidence and motivation.

Regaining control of your home and life is a transformative experience.

It's much more than the simple act of decluttering.

It's Space Making.

What is Space Making?

Simply put, the goal of Space Making is to make space for what you love.

Space Making does involve decluttering and organizing, but it's more than both of these things. Why? Because Space Making is highly focused on the individual. It is highly focused on you.

Space Making means...

- creating the best home for you, not a magazine cover

- deciding what to keep and how much to keep; you don't let anyone else pressure you one way or another

- building your own rules as you go along instead of following someone else's rules because only you know what works best for you and your family

- getting clear about your personal motivations for transforming your space

- prioritizing sustainability, either in terms of being environmentally responsible or in terms of decluttering for long-lasting results, or both

- thinking honestly about your past as you better understand your home and your clutter, and purposefully aiming toward a brighter future

What I want you to understand up front is that Space Making is not *just* the act of getting rid of things. It's the careful curation of your home with a clear purpose.

Your purpose is unique to you. Let me ask you, "What would you do if the clutter was gone? How would you use that space?"

Would you have an arts and craft room, a cozy reading nook, a workout zone, a walk-in closet, an empty garage to park your car in, clean counter tops to cook on? Maybe you'd have space to entertain guests, space to display your most treasured possessions, space to relax, room to breathe.

The state of your mind is directly linked to the state of your home. If we can calm the chaos in your home, that sense of calm will affect every aspect of your life.

The Rules of Space Making

Before we dive headfirst into your home transformation, we need to establish a few rules. Even if they seem strange at first, I promise you'll thank me later.

Here are the simple rules of Space Making:

1. Don't Buy Anything... Yet

2. Don't Make Decisions Based on Guilt (No Shoulding!)

3. Avoid Arbitrary Rules, Develop Your Own Instead

4. Be Open to Change

5. Lighten Up!

Rule #1 Don't Buy Anything...Yet

Until you reach the **After** stage, don't buy anything. This includes but is not limited to: organizers, furniture, home decor, kitchen accessories, or anything you think may be a fun accessory for decluttering. For now, consider yourself on a temporary **Buy Ban**.

Why?

Thinking you can fix your clutter problem with a new bookshelf or storage cabinet is wishful thinking. It's an obvious attempt to skip from the **Before** to the **After** without having to go through the **During**.

It is highly likely that after you finish decluttering, you won't need what you thought you did. Your home will transform as you do this work and you may find you don't need that new console table after all.

But there's another, less obvious reason for the **Buy Ban**. I see this all the time: most people don't realize how many organizers and how much home decor they already have because it's hiding in the clutter. My clients are always especially shocked by how many organizers we uncover as we declutter, and without fail, we always have leftovers in the end.

When you make it to the **After** you can buy whatever you need. What's more, you can buy with confidence knowing that the new pieces will fit perfectly in your new space.

Only on rare occasions are there exceptions to this rule. I've had clients who were on a time crunch so they purchased some key pieces of furniture before the project began. If you do this, always keep your receipts just in case!

Rule #2 No "Shoulding"!

Shoulding
   [SHood-ing]
   verb
   modal verb: shoulding

1. **"Shoulding on yourself."** Doing what you think you should do instead of what you want to do.

Example #1
Friend #1: "Do you want to keep this dress?"
Friend #2: "Well, I don't wear it but my sister gave it to me. So I should keep it."
Friend #1: "Stop shoulding on yourself!"

Example #2
Friend #1: "I really don't like this tea set, but my Mom gave it to me as a souvenir from her vacation so I should keep it so that I don't hurt her feelings."
Friend #2: "Stop shoulding on yourself!"

2. **"Shoulding on others."** Telling someone else what they should or shouldn't do.

Example #1
You: "I'm finished!"
Stranger: "You should declutter more clothes. I don't see why you need so many sweaters."
You: "Stop shoulding on me! I love sweaters!"

Example #2
Stranger: "You should only keep 3 pairs of shoes."
You: "You don't know me, stop shoulding on me!"

Why?

Keeping or decluttering something based on someone else's opinion is not confident decluttering. This is your home and you're the one who has to live with these decisions. No **Shoulding** on yourself or others.

Rule #3 Avoid Arbitrary Rules, Develop Your Own Instead

You know those random decluttering rules that you hear from time to time?

"If you haven't worn it in 6 months, donate it."

"Don't keep books you've already read."

"Donate all the books, get a Kindle!"

"You only need 2 plates and 2 bowls."

"Don't keep 'just in case' items."

"Get rid of all duplicates"

From now on, I want you to forget those rules.

Why?

I'm not a fan of arbitrary decluttering rules because they tend to encourage a short term approach to decluttering.

Rules like this encourage you to be ruthless to the point of being wasteful. They encourage you to let go of things like a pair of dress shoes that you keep for rare occasions such as weddings or interviews. But what happens if you suddenly find yourself on the job market two years later? You're going to need those shoes, but you decluttered them. So what do you do? You buy another pair.

The most effective form of decluttering happens when you know yourself and your space so well that you build the rules to fit. Of course this is harder to do because it requires critical thinking, but that's exactly what I'm going to help you do in this book.

Your own rules will fit you best and they'll last a lifetime.

Rule #4 Be Open to Change

You're not simply decluttering, you're changing your entire life and transforming it into something calmer and clearer. But it doesn't come for free. This new life will require you to drop old habits and adopt new ones. All I ask is that you keep an open mind throughout the process. Be open to change!

Why?

As you declutter and get more acquainted with the behaviors that have gotten you to the point you're at today, you'll eventually meet a fork in the road that requires a pivotal decision. "Will I continue repeating the same patterns that led me here, or will I choose a new path?"

Old habits die hard, right? I'm not asking you to transform overnight. What I am asking is that you open yourself up now to the idea that change is coming.

Take this rule and file it away in your brain somewhere for safe keeping. No need to access the file now, but keep it available so you are ready when the time comes.

Rule #5 Lighten Up!

This process is hard. Don't make it harder than it needs to be. Lighten up!

Why?

When you create an environment that is light-hearted and full of spontaneous laughter, you're creating an atmosphere that you want to work in. And hey, if your declutter buddies are having fun, maybe they'll want to come back and help you again!

When you find a 20-year-old spice container in your cabinet or seven open jars of strawberry jam in your refrigerator, don't let yourself slide too deeply into negative self-talk: "I'm a terrible person. I can't believe I let this happen." Remember that we're all doing our best. It's not the end of the world.

But I'm not saying to let yourself off the hook either. Your refrigerator became so cluttered that you unknowingly bought seven jars of the same jam. And now they're all moldy! I think we can all agree that this isn't a good thing. But instead of beating yourself up, take a moment to make a mental note so that you don't find yourself in this situation again.

But do laugh about it. I mean, it's a little funny, right? Seven jars of identical jam. It makes me curious to know how many pieces of toast you eat for breakfast each morning. Laugh and move on. Or maybe stop to eat a piece of toast.

Be intentional about embedding pockets of fun into your declutter. Start the morning with a coffee run to your favorite cafe. Put on your favorite movie, podcast, or YouTube channel while you work. Take a minute to try on those old clothes from the 80s. Actions like these are valuable even if they slow your progress a tiny bit.

Even if you forget the first four Rules of Space Making, remember this one: Lighten Up!

Let's Begin!

This book is organized in a very straightforward way. It's designed to take you from the beginning of your Space Maker journey to the end, guiding you every step along the way.

In fact, one of the things my clients love most about my method is how simple it is. There are three stages and each one is clearly defined.

Stage 1: The Before
Stage 2: The During
Stage 3: The After

I promise that if you follow each step of the process, sincerely, at your own pace, this journey will transform more than just your home.

It will change your life.

The Oath of a Space Maker

Now you know what this book is about. You know that a journey awaits you.

If you're serious about changing your life, I'll need you to take the Space Maker oath before you begin.

Hand over heart and repeat after me:

"I, (insert name here)
Promise you
That no matter how slow my progress,
I will not give up.
I will trust the process.
Even when it looks like a stampede of wild horses ran through my home,
Even when I want to curl into a ball and cry,
I will not quit.
Finally, I promise to take back all the mean things I will say about April in the **During**.
This I swear."

The Before

Introduction to Stage 1: The Before

This is where your Space Making journey begins. The **Before** is the most important stage of the declutter journey, but it's also the part that other methods tend to gloss over or skip altogether.

The purpose of decluttering is to make space for the things you love. Like cleaning out your craft room so you can finally sew that quilt you promised you'd get around to, or clearing off the countertops to get your holiday bake on. There are countless reasons to create more space through the act of decluttering and it's this hope of change that motivates us to get started.

So it's understandable why, in an attempt to create this new space, many people jump directly into the physical act of removing clutter from their home. Doing this makes you feel good. It makes you feel like you're making progress. However, it doesn't address the deep-seated emotions or the underlying cause behind the clutter.

I don't want to give you a bandaid fix. I want to help you uncover the source of your clutter so that you can move forward with long lasting results. The hard-earned triumph of real change in your home and in yourself—this is the aim of Space Making.

Chapter 1
Take the Pressure Off by Setting Realistic Expectations

Staying up late to watch "Design On A Dime" with my Mom will always be one of my favorite pastimes. I love home makeover shows and I love seeing the **Before** and **After** shots, but it's important to remember that these shows are designed for entertainment. If you base your expectations on what you see in these shows, you'll be setting yourself up for failure before you even begin.

TV Homeowner: "I can't believe we did this makeover in 1 week!"

REALITY: The production crew has a team of professionals working full-time on a single project. A team of strong men can carry the heavy things while a team of designers can brainstorm solutions. And don't worry about cooking during this makeover. The food will be catered!

You are just one person. You might be working a full time job and raising a family at the same time. You might be caring for a loved one or dealing with any number of real-world difficulties.

Your progress might be slow. Be patient with yourself.

TV: The **Before** images are the worst part. It's all uphill from here.

REALITY: If only that were the case!

Your home will get worse before it gets better. This messy part of a home transformation is rarely shown on the screen, but it is a normal part of the process.

TV: The final look resembles a magazine photoshoot.

REALITY: Your final home looks brighter and cleaner and more beautiful, but it still looks like a real home where real people live.

I'm always curious where they hide real peoples' stuff in these "**After**" shots. Like, where is the surplus stock of toilet paper and the mountain of mismatched plates? What about the obnoxiously colored cat tunnels and the dirty clothes hamper? How will this home look a month after the production crew leaves?

TV: "We only have a small, $20,000 budget for this project." - this is an actual quote from a Netflix show.

REALITY: Do I even need to talk about how out of touch this is for most people around the world?

I don't want you comparing yourself and your progress to anything that you see on the screen. Even the makeovers you see on YouTube are productions at the end of the day (mine included). If you let even an ounce of comparison sneak in, it's likely to leave you feeling disappointed in your own home transformation.

So leave your unrealistic expectations behind and set some realistic expectations:

1. Decluttering is Therapy

2. It Takes Multiple Passes to Declutter

3. It's Going To Get Worse Before it Gets Better

4. Sometimes You're Not Ready

Realistic Expectation #1 - Decluttering is Therapy

A long-lasting decluttering effort is like therapy. It's a journey of understanding how your past and your future collide. It's a process that requires deep and honest personal assessment as you seek to understand yourself and your home more clearly. It's not just decluttering, it's **Declutter Therapy**.

In the spirit of understanding I want to share a bit of my personal journey with you. It's a story about why I am the way I am and how all the twists and turns of my early adulthood turned out to be fundamental in shaping the Space Maker Method.

I did my undergrad in Portland, Oregon. I was an indecisive 20-something with a vague idea of what I wanted in life, bouncing through majors as if I wasn't wasting thousands of dollars with each new decision.

I started in business because I was confident I wanted to be an entrepreneur. But that grew boring and eventually I moved to the education department because I enjoyed teaching, or thought I did, until the in-classroom work began.

Then in my junior year, my college suddenly closed! I needed to find somewhere else to get a diploma.

My college closing down turned out to be a blessing in disguise, as many rough moments do. I ended up at a new university with yet another new career trajectory. I eventually graduated with a bachelor's degree in Human Development, the branch of psychology that studies how people grow and change throughout their lives.

Human development was a perfect blend of my passion and natural talent. Helping others live more fulfilling lives by understanding themselves better and learning to communicate more effectively—that was a life purpose I could stand behind. I was even planning to further my degree with a masters in Marriage and Family Therapy.

But soon after graduating I traveled overseas for the first time. I got a taste of the real world and realized that I knew absolutely nothing about the real world. How naive was I to think I could enlighten others when I myself knew so little? In some ways, travel became my education from that point on, and I've been living overseas ever since.

Ironically, I actually did become a teacher (in South Korea) for a number of those years. I worked with young children, so my Human Development studies proved to be as useful as my education studies.

But why on earth am I telling you all this? I wanted to give you a little glimpse into my life, and my past, so that you can better understand who I am. I hope it helps you understand why the Space Maker Method is the way it is. It's a mix of my tough-but-compassionate teaching style, my natural interest in decluttering and organizing, and my passion for understanding people in hopes that they can better understand themselves. It's all of those things, colored by a traveler's appreciation for the wide diversity of human experience.

And so, in that same spirit of understanding, I don't want you to move through your declutter journey by casually discarding items without much thought. Instead, I want you to understand yourself and why your clutter has gotten out of control in the first place. I want you to explore the feelings, thoughts, and emotions you've subconsciously attached to your possessions over the years. I want you to connect the dots throughout your history of behavior, taking your environment into consideration and examining the choices you've made that have contributed to the state of your home today. I hope that during your journey you will be brave enough to bring your mental junk into the light and give it a good examination, just as you would with your physical junk.

This is how you move forward. Not only by removing clutter from your home, but also by gripping the steering wheel of your life story.

You're charting a new course for your future, but remember to be patient with yourself along the way, as patient as a therapist. Because you're not just decluttering, you're also engaging in **Declutter Therapy**.

Story Time

While decluttering my parents' home for the first time, I kept coming across these itty bitty clay figurines. To most people they would have looked like unnecessary clutter collecting dust on a shelf. They weren't even well-made. They looked cheap.

When it came time for my mom and I to work on the bookshelf that the figurines were on, I asked her if she wanted to keep them. I hadn't even finished my sentence before she quickly responded, "Yes!" Her sharp tone gave me fair warning to drop the subject. I wanted to ask questions but I could tell from her response that it was not the right time, so I put the figurines back on the shelf and moved on.

A few days later as we were decluttering a new area, she shared her revelation with tearful eyes. "I know why I can't let the figurines go. They remind me of Josh. He made them for me when he was little. Crafts were a special bond we shared. I felt so special that he made them for me."

To anyone else they were just clay figurines made by a child, but to her they were a sacred memory of her nephew, my younger cousin, who had suddenly passed the year before. My mom was still navigating her grief at that moment, and was unable to

> *detach her grief from the physical form of the figurines. Nor did she have to.*
>
> *To an onlooker it might appear that we made no progress in that moment. After all, we left the figurines on the bookshelf. But we did move forward in that moment because my mom, for the first time, became aware of how emotionally intertwined she was to those clay figures. This self-awareness is essential. It is the foundation for growth, for change, for forward movement.*
>
> *Our homes and the items within tell a story. I want you to have the realistic expectation that you may need time to unravel all the hidden layers of that story.*

Realistic Expectation #2 - It Takes Multiple Passes to Declutter

One of the most common complaints I see on my declutter videos on YouTube is that someone watching from afar is disappointed about the fact that more items weren't decluttered on our first pass through the home. But true decluttering doesn't happen in one go. It takes **Multiple Passes**.

Many people have lived in their homes for years or even decades. One round of decluttering simply isn't enough to sort through generations of clutter and emotional baggage. If you could do it in one pass, that would be magical. But for most people this is just a ridiculous expectation to place on yourself and others.

The good news is you'll grow more confident in your decision-making with each pass. You may find, for example, that during the first pass you're unable to let go of as much as you'd like. Don't think your efforts were in vain, because after that first pass, you'll be thinking about your clutter in a new way. Your brain will work on some of those tough decisions while you sleep and while you go about your week. Eventually you'll be energized for another round of decluttering, and with each pass you will curate with more clarity.

Each pass is a victory because you will lighten your load AND strengthen your **Declutter Muscles**, all while moving closer to your desired result.

Realistic Expectation #3 - It's Going To Get Worse Before it Gets Better

When you start your decluttering journey, it's only natural to assume that with each day, your home will get progressively better. "This is the worst it's ever going to be," you tell yourself. Well, I hate to be the bearer of bad news, but I need to be honest with you. Things are going to get worse.

When I first started decluttering on YouTube I received plenty of comments that said something to the effect of, "You need to stop, you're just making it worse!" But creating more chaos is a natural part of the process. We have to tear it all down to start to rebuild.

The good news is if you have this expectation from the beginning, then you'll be less likely to get discouraged when things get messy.

It's also important to remember that even if *you* understand that temporary chaos is part of the process, the shared occupants of your space may not. I've had more than a few partners and roommates come home, shocked by the amount of stuff being decluttered and how it seemed to be taking over the home.

Let everyone in your home know what to expect before it happens so that you can all stay cool, calm, and collected. If the stress or change of scenery is something they are uneasy about, talk it out. Discuss ways to ease the friction. Perhaps someone in your home is going through a stressful time at work, so you agree to wait a couple weeks until things calm down. You could set specific dates for your project, or you could agree to confine the chaos to certain zones within the house, marking them off limits until you're done.

There will be moments of chaos. Not just for whoever is leading the declutter, but for everyone who lives under the same roof.

Realistic Expectation #4 - Sometimes You're Not Ready

I don't want you (or anyone for that matter) to start your Space Making journey before you're ready. Forced or rushed decluttering can easily lead to feelings of resentment and regret.

What if, instead, you waited until that moment when you could say with 100% confidence: "I'm ready!" Or maybe, "I'm so tired of this s*** I just want to throw it all away!! $%@!!!!"

I like this! Actually I love when you're frustrated and angry about the clutter because then I know you'll be ready to do the work required to create change.

If you aren't mentally ready to start... just WAIT. Give yourself time to think, time to grieve, time to get through a stressful season of life. Give yourself time to develop a clear vision of what you want for your space. Start to dream about that glorious future. In time you'll grow more and more irritated by the clutter. Then one day, when you are truly ready, you will be a force and no clutter will be safe from your donation bin!

Chapter 2
Examine Your Clutter by Performing a Walk Through

Now that we've set some realistic expectations for your project, it's time to address your clutter.

The main goal of this next step is to bring awareness to the clutter. If you've been avoiding your stuff, or pretending it doesn't exist, now is the time to face it.

No shame or guilt allowed. We're just going to look at what's going on, similar to how a doctor examines a patient. We're going to be calm and dispassionate and try and view the clutter from an outsider's perspective.

One of the easiest ways to do this is to enlist the help of a family member or friend. Ideally this would be someone who doesn't live with you, someone you can trust who can also hold you accountable. As an outsider they are unattached to your belongings. They may raise questions or come to conclusions that you never would have considered. Together you can make a rational assessment of your space.

Remember, we are not decluttering yet! But we are getting active. We are bravely assessing the clutter and starting to ask questions that normally go unasked.

Here are the steps to performing a **Walk Through**:

1. Take Photos of Your Stuff

2. Notice Hot Spots

3. Ask Questions

4. Explore the Root Cause of the Clutter

Step #1 - Take Photos of Your Stuff

As we go through the **Walk Through** it's a great idea to take photos of each space. No need to get fancy with it, these are just for you. Snap photos of the space as it is right now. As scary as it might seem in the moment, you will feel extremely proud later when you get to compare your progress photos. These photos can be an excellent source of motivation for you along the way. During those moments when you feel like you aren't making progress, or like you want to quit, you can look back on your **Before** images and realize how far you've come.

I recommend saving your photos to a folder in your phone immediately after snapping. You can even label it "Space Making!" This will make it easy to add photos as you go along. As the folder grows it will document the story of your Space Making journey.

Step #2 - Notice Hot Spots

Stand at your front door and begin walking through all the areas of your home.

As you go along, I want you to observe how a room, a drawer, or a cabinet makes you feel - both mentally and physically. Do you feel calm when you look at it? Does it stress you out? Do you think to yourself,

- "Why do I even have this stuff?"

- "I wish I could just trash everything."

- "This is so embarrassing."

A **Hot Spot** could be an area that is out-of-control messy, but it could also be an area or item with sensitive emotional attachment, such as a box of old photographs, or a closet with clothing items from a parent who has passed away.

Some areas and items are obviously sensitive, but others are emotionally charged in more subtle ways. Maybe you've been avoiding decluttering the coffee mugs due to the memories and feelings they evoke. Maybe you've been steering clear of a certain room for reasons that you haven't quite articulated to yourself. These areas will likely require more time and patience, but try your best to make a note of them as you pass through.

If you do notice a few spots that are especially "hot", write them down. If your entire home is stressful, keep it simple and write down the top 1 - 5 areas that are the most difficult. You can reference these notes later when we decide where to start.

Don't dwell on the **Hot Spots**. Just take a mental and/or physical note and keep on walking.

Step #3 - Ask Questions

I want to give you an idea of some of the questions you can ask yourself while observing your clutter. The goal of these questions is to help you understand your space more. I want you to be able to communicate your goals, needs, and restrictions.

If you have a helper, this can be a fantastic way to get on the same page about the project and set realistic expectations about the work that needs to be done.

Think of these questions as cues to get the conversation rolling. You may want to adjust them, or expand on them, based on the specific needs of your family and your home.

1. Why do you want to declutter?

2. Are you nervous to declutter? Why?

3. Can you identify the biggest problem areas in your home?

4. Which space causes you the most anxiety?

5. What area would create the most impactful change for you?

6. How do you specifically use this space? Give me a

run-down of how you come through the door after work. Where do you put your bags, coats, keys, bills, etc?

7. What designated areas could you create to help you stay more organized?

8. What unique characteristics of your home do we need to consider?

9. What are you ready to declutter?

10. What are you not ready to declutter?

11. How does your space make you feel currently?

12. What space do you anticipate will be the most emotional for you?

13. Is this a shared space? Are you both ready to declutter? Or do we need to find a compromise?

14. What are the individual needs of each person who interacts with the space?

15. What would help you live most comfortably in your space?

16. What is your end goal?

17. How much time do you have to work towards your goal each week?

18. What changes are you willing to make to achieve your goal?

These questions will get you started. You can adjust them as needed, but the point is to get curious about your space and start asking questions.

Step #4 - Explore the Root Cause of the Clutter

If you really want to fix the clutter once and for all, you need to get to the heart of why it's happening. You need to find your **Clutter Cause**—the underlying cause of your clutter.

You can start by asking yourself, "Why is this clutter here in the first place?"

I know it sounds simple, but you'd be surprised how many people skip this step and jump right into the physical act of removing items from their home. This one question is the gateway to uncovering the cause behind your clutter, but we need to be clear about a couple of things.

First of all, the goal of this exercise is to understand *your* **Clutter Cause**, no one else's. This is not the time for excuses. It's not the time for blame. This is your transformation.

I've done more than a few **Walk Throughs** with clients who are quick to put the blame on their spouse (especially when the spouse isn't around). For example, if we're looking at a messy space, their first response might be, "These are my partner's tools. They're just exploding and taking up so much room!" While that may very well be the case, from my experience with clients, the main issue is usually not their partner's toolbox. It may be contributing to the chaos, but it's not the sole reason things are out of control. Most often there are other "explosions" going on that don't have anything to do with their partner. Of course, it's easier to blame someone else than to be honest about the portion of blame that belongs to you.

To be clear, I'm not saying that you need to take full responsibility for everything, even when it's not yours to take. I just don't want you getting too hung up on things you can't control. Everyone else's transformation is up to them and will happen on a different timeline.

But now that we are only focused on *your* **Clutter Cause**, I want you to start thinking about your life as a story. What happened in your past, and what is happening right now, that is contributing to the clutter?

Most of my clients can list one or two stressful life events that directly contributed to their clutter problem, whether it's a new job, a new child, a medical diagnosis, the loss of a loved one, or some kind of random catastrophe.

Maybe you used to be an organized person, but with the stress of change, you've had no energy to tidy. Without regular maintenance, the mess compounded, and it was all so frustrating that you ignored it instead of doing something about it. These kinds of stories actually make me hopeful. An organized person can be an organized person again, they might just need some help and encouragement to get there.

But some of you might be thinking, "I haven't had any big life events! This is just how I've always been." That statement also speaks volumes and probably means that we're going to need to spend more time uncovering the cause of your clutter.

Maybe you don't like cleaning up after yourself and you neglect all sorts of regular home maintenance. Or maybe you don't know how. Maybe you're living alone for the first time and you've never been taught how to keep an orderly home. It could be that you learned this messy behavior from your parents, having grown up in the home of a hoarder. Or maybe you're simply not proud of your home, so you feel like, "What's the point?" Maybe you get distracted easily. Maybe you have a shopping addiction.

There are many potential underlying reasons for the state of your home. My hope is that as you focus on your **Clutter Cause**, you'll start to connect the dots and see how those issues manifest themselves in your clutter.

This sort of self-knowledge is empowering. Once you know your **Clutter Cause**, you'll be able to make changes that actually last.

***

Bonus Tip: Give Yourself a Break!

The hidden power of understanding your **Clutter Cause** *is that it allows you to give yourself a little more compassion. We humans can be pretty hard on ourselves, especially when it comes to self-talk. Guilt can add to the stress of our cluttered spaces and spread into other areas of our lives.*

But if you can be more compassionate with yourself as you observe your clutter, you might be able to take the edge off of your fears and anxieties. Then, with a little more mental space for hope and confidence, you can summon the strength to start tackling your clutter, day by day, piece by piece.

Lastly, don't feel pressure to find your **Clutter Cause** *overnight! You will peel back the layers of understanding as you go. This is* **Declutter Therapy***, after all. But you've begun asking questions, and that's good enough for now. That's exactly where you should be as you complete your* **Walk Through***.*

Chapter 3
Guarantee Success with Motivation & Accountability

You're embarking on a journey and the very best fuel for this journey is motivation. If your motivation is strong enough then you will reach the finish line.

I want to give you a personalized tool to help remind you of your motivation all throughout this journey. This tool is called a **Compass Question**, and you can think of it as a "motivation mantra."

Create a Compass Question

A **Compass Question** is a personalized statement or question that you can use as a guide to make tough decisions. The catch is that YOU have to be the one who chooses the question in order for it to actually work. It has to resonate with you.

Here are some examples of **Compass Questions**.

- Am I going to miss this?

- Does this make me happy?

- Do I really need this?

- Do I want to carry this into the next chapter of my life?

- Does this make me anxious?

I find that when I suggest a few of these questions to my clients, they will usually latch onto one of them and also give it a personalized twist that makes it their own.

The best **Compass Questions** have a personalized twist that makes them unique to your life story. They motivate you by keeping you focused on a brighter future.

For example…

- Will this empower me to live my best life?

- Do I want to carry this into my retirement?

- Do I really need this now that my kids have moved out?

- Will this ease my anxiety and create a peaceful environment?

- For my upcoming year of health and self-love, will this help me?

- Does this serve my new life?

- Is this item coming with me into my dream future? Or is it keeping me in the past?

For all those times when you don't know whether to keep something or let it go, allow your **Compass Question** to guide you. Not only will it help you make difficult decisions, but It will also remind you of your personal motivations for Space Making.

***

Story Time

My very first client was a woman who lived alone in a small, city apartment. Her space was overflowing with clutter and needed lots of help.

In her first email she said, "I want to change the whole mood of my home." And as we decluttered together for over a month, I learned more about her personal journey.

"5 years ago I lost my mom to breast cancer and I became depressed," she told me, "I was so neglectful of my own well-being that I started skipping my regular health checkups, and eventually I was diagnosed with breast cancer myself." Her own battle with cancer took years, but she was finally cancer-free. The doctor

had just declared her to be in a state of complete remission. Not long after that, she reached out to me for help in her home.

Her **Compass Question** was, "Will this promote health and well-being in my life going forward?" Because her question resonated deeply with her personal story, it helped her make difficult decisions and it also helped motivate her during our long work hours.

Using her favorite books and comfiest chair we created a cozy reading/relaxation nook by the window overlooking the city. Instead of getting rid of her unused exercise bike, we dusted it off and created a pleasant workout zone around it. She kept the clothes that made her feel the best. She kept the things in her kitchen that promoted health and readily discarded everything else. Every change we made emphasized health and self-care for her future.

On our last day together she told me, "My home has been a disaster for so long. I've been so stressed. I've been alone in my home for far too long because I was too embarrassed by it. But now, after getting good news from my doctor I'm so excited to invite my friends over to a space I'm proud of and celebrate being cancer free!"

Establish Accountability

Accountability is like backup motivation. When someone else knows about your efforts and your dreams, they can give you the boost you need to keep going.

Nothing is more powerful than having a friend or family member in the room with you as you declutter. You can cheer each other on. Keep each other on task. Take a snack break together when needed.

If possible, I recommend getting help from someone who doesn't live under the same roof. They'll see your clutter more objectively and they'll ask questions you may not expect—as we discussed in the **Walk Through** chapter. Setting times to meet will create focused periods of work. You'll have to schedule decluttering dates on the calendar instead of just leaving it to chance and hoping you'll get around to it one day. (Personally I love **Coffee and Clutter** dates! Bribe me with coffee and of course I'll be down to declutter. Just give me a dark roast please.)

A family member or roommate can help as well—anyone who can help physically or simply be present as an emotional support partner! Just remember the fourth rule of Space Making: Lighten up! The more fun your helper has, the more likely they are to keep helping you.

Even scheduling a phone date or video call with a friend will add a new level of accountability and enjoyment to your work.

But what if you're alone and want to get motivated to declutter?

You can watch some decluttering videos @SpaceMakerMethod on YouTube for a boost of motivation and accountability!

I know I'm doing a bit of self-promotion here, but hear me out. The people who watch my YouTube channel are not just passive viewers. Every single week I see comments like this on my videos:

> *"I'm decluttering my kitchen as I watch this video. Thanks for the motivation!"*

> *"Love listening to you guys chatting as I declutter my own bedroom."*

> *"Sunday morning is my time to work in my home. I put on the new Space Maker video and away I go!"*

> *"I got so motivated that I had to pause this video and take some things to the donation center!"*

So even if you don't have a friend or family member who is willing/able to come to your home, you can find a lot of support from the Space Maker community online. I'm extremely proud of this community because everyone is incredibly compassionate, intelligent, and supportive.

Feel free to leave a comment and tell people what you're up to. Or simply watch one of my clients transforming their home until you get so motivated that you run off and do some Space Making of your own!

Let's Begin

This completes the **Before** stage of the Space Maker Method. Though these tasks seem simple, they are crucial for a successful decluttering effort.

First of all, you set realistic expectations for your project. You know:

- You should have patience and compassion for yourself as you engage in **Declutter Therapy.**

- Your home will need **Multiple Passes** of decluttering.

- You can stay calm when things get worse before they get better because it's all part of the process.

- You should start when you're ready, not before.

In your **Walk Through**, you came face to face with your clutter, choosing to no longer let it intimidate you. You began to ask questions in order to better understand the root of the clutter. It might take time to find your **Clutter Cause**, but the point is not to have it all figured out right now; the point is to start asking questions.

And finally, to keep yourself motivated throughout the **Messy Middle**, you created a **Compass Question** and established accountability. You did all of these things before you even decluttered a single item.

Now that we've done our mental prep, it's time to roll up our sleeves and get to work.

The During

Introduction to Stage 2: The During

The concept of the **During** was a revelation for me.

I've always been annoyed or at least amused by the unrealistic nature of the "before and after" culture of home makeovers on TV. I always knew that something was missing. But I didn't truly understand the power of the **During** until I started working in people's homes.

You see, before and after photos are fun to look at. They are inspirational and sexy. They attract clicks and views. But when it comes to helping real people in real homes, what people need help with is everything in between. How ironic that the in-between stuff, the most important part of the process, doesn't have a name.

I was amazed at how my YouTube audience embraced this idea once I started emphasizing it. They even started sending me their **During** photos. Actually, I asked for their Space Making photos and the **During** was what they were most excited to share. They sent me photos of their messy bedrooms, chaotic kitchens, piles of clothes on the living room sofa. They told me inspirational stories of how they were making progress, slowly but surely. We encouraged each other to "embrace the **During**" and not be afraid of the **Messy Middle**.

What was going on? Were we all just being lazy? Were we throwing progress out the window and reveling in our messes?

Exactly the opposite. Here's what was happening: real people were sharing their progress—however big or small—and realizing they weren't alone in their struggles. We were taking the shame out of the home transformation process, telling each other it's okay to make a mess as long as you're actively decluttering and making small, incremental wins. Together we were shattering the unrealistic expectation that every time you try to improve your home, you have to achieve Hollywood-level results or else you were a failure.

The idea of "embracing the **During**" helps people get started, even people who've been trying to start for years. Even more importantly, it helps them stay focused while decluttering instead of getting overwhelmed and giving up.

Chapter 4
Simplify the Starting Process: Start Here!

In all my years of doing this work, I've learned that there are two great dangers to decluttering.

1. "I don't know where to start."

2. "I can get started, but eventually I get overwhelmed and quit."

So let's prep for success. Let's not be surprised when these issues arise.

Right now I want to address problem #1 (Pretty soon we'll address problem #2).

I want you to know that everybody feels anxious at the start. You are not alone. That's why the Space Maker Method is designed to make the task of "getting started" as easy as possible.

Here are five easy ways to get started:

1. Quick Win

2. Greatest Impact

3. Unlock

4. Find the Floor

5. Tried and True

I encourage you to choose the one that makes you the most excited. Choose the one that seems so easy and simple that you might as well just go ahead and do it.

Getting started is a massive victory, and that's all you have to do right now. Don't worry about your home's design. Don't worry about organization. Don't worry about anything except taking that first step.

The Quick Win

Declutter projects are overwhelming, especially in the beginning. It's best to break it down into manageable pieces instead of trying to tackle everything at once.

To do this I like to start with a **Quick Win**.

A **Quick Win** can be a small room or a designated space within a room, but it has to be a small project. It has to be something you can knock out in a single afternoon. Or less. It could be an hour or even ten minutes.

Here are some examples of **Quick Wins**:

- a junk drawer
- the bathroom cabinets
- your closet
- clothing piles
- linen closet
- a bookshelf
- one shelf on a bookshelf
- the pile of clothes on the bookshelf
- a doom pile
- a category within your closet (shoes, handbags, underwear, etc...)
- a corner of a room
- the pile of papers by the front door
- the laundry room
- Christmas decorations
- the spice shelf

- the refrigerator

- the entryway

- a small chunk of the mountain of clutter in the bedroom

- a basket of stuff

This small project is your secret weapon, not because of the physical progress you make but because of the mental impact it has on you. First of all, you got started. Second of all, you *finished something*. The impossible has become possible—the effect this has on your confidence can not be overstated.

Never underestimate the power of a **Quick Win**.

The Greatest Impact

You can think of the **Greatest Impact** as the area that—if you got it under control—would have the most transformative mental or physical impact on your life.

The **Greatest Impact** area is unique to your home and your story, something I hope you can identify as you do your **Walk Through** and ask pointed questions that dig deeper into understanding your home.

If you're helping someone who wants to take action but is still a bit skeptical, this can be a great way to win them over because it creates serious, life-changing results right away.

Here are a few examples of the **Greatest Impact**.

Let's say you struggle every morning to get ready for work. Your closet is a mess. You can never find the clothes you need. When you try to grab a pair of jeans, accessories slide down on your head like an avalanche.

In this situation, starting your project by creating a calm closet could set the tone for a better, less stressful day. Even if the rest of your home is still a mess, that one closet could have a huge impact on your life. It could be the motivation you need to keep working through the rest of your home.

Let's look at another example. Let's consider someone who is struggling with their health. Let's say that for this person, eating a healthy diet is of utmost importance and urgency.

Starting this person's declutter in the kitchen could have the greatest immediate impact on their life. Maybe they'll actually enjoy being in the kitchen when plastic lids aren't cascading down from every cabinet. Looking for ingredients will be fun when they are well-organized and none of them are expired. Digging through the fridge won't be a scary adventure anymore. The countertops will be clean and clutter-free, ready for meal prep!

When a space is chaotic we tend to avoid it. Is there a space in your home that would totally change your life if, instead of dreading it, you actually enjoyed it?

The **Greatest Impact** isn't always a room or a specific space, either. It could be a category like papers, art supplies, or clothes that are overwhelming your space. It could be anything that is uniquely important to your home and situation.

For example, if you or someone you're helping uses a mobility-assistive device, then safety within the home is of critical importance. If the sheer amount of clutter is restricting safe passageways to and from certain areas of the house, this should be dealt with right away. Creating larger pathways and eliminating tripping hazards from the most frequented paths could eliminate potential disasters down the road. No matter what else needs to be done, in situations like this I find it best to use tunnel vision. Let's focus on health and safety first, we can worry about clothes later.

Ask yourself, "What would have the biggest effect on my life if I got control of it today?" This won't always be the easiest place to start, but the results will be powerful.

The Unlock

Sometimes when a project is complicated enough, what you really need is a way to unlock it.

The **Unlock** is the area or room that the rest of the home depends on. It's often a closet, a garage, a storage room, or some place where many items are stored. It's rarely the most desirable place to start, but practically speaking, it's the best.

When decluttering an entire home feels like a giant puzzle, the **Unlock** is the piece that helps all the other pieces fall into place.

***

Story Time

I worked in an apartment in Miami that was severely damaged in Hurricane Irma. (This was a 5-episode series on my YouTube channel.) The apartment had flood damage and needed professional help. After finally securing a contractor, my clients spent two years shuffling from room to room as each space got renovated. By the end of the construction years they were understandably exhausted. They decided to accept the chaos and "live with it forever" as they told me.

As I walked through their apartment I thought, "Oh ya, this totally makes sense." I could see how their shower ended up full of construction materials, and why there were boxes of unused tiles in the corner of the living room. But it wasn't immediately clear where we should start.

It would have been great to enjoy a **Quick Win** by getting all of the leftover construction materials out of the shower. However, we had no place to put those materials. (We couldn't dispose of them because renovations were still ongoing.) They did have a separate storage room in the apartment building, which was the only sensible place to store things, but it was so full that we

> *couldn't add anything to it.*
>
> *Eventually we decided that we had to make space in the storage room before we could do anything else. There was really no way around it. It certainly was not exciting to begin their project by lifting heavy items in a dark room, but that's exactly what we did. The storage room was our **Unlock**, and the rest of the project flowed smoothly from there.*

Find the Floor

This is one of my all time favorites, something I've been practicing since childhood. I love this option because similar to the **Quick Win**, it provides an immediate sense of satisfaction.

Find the Floor is just like it sounds: start by finding the floor. There's no room for confusion or misunderstanding. All of the clutter on the floor should be relocated. Pick up the trash around the bookshelf, the laundry by the bed, the contents of your purse that you dumped out—all of it. Relocate it to a table top, bed, countertop, sofa... anywhere that's not the floor.

It's up to you if you want to declutter what's on the floor as you go, or simply relocate everything and then start sorting when you're done. Personally, I prefer the latter.

This is such an easy place to start because the quicker you can see the floor, the lighter you're going to feel. Logistically speaking, it will be easier for you to walk around the room as you work. If you want, you can even stop to vacuum or mop the space before addressing the relocated piles. This will give you an even greater sense of satisfaction and progress.

At times it won't be possible to **Find the Floor** in one go. There may be far too many things. You may be too overwhelmed by the mountain of stuff. You may start tilting into a panic attack just by looking at it. In this case, do your best to look as objectively as possible at the area. What type of items do you see most? Books? Clothes? Shoes? Papers? Trash? Start by identifying one category at a time and removing it from the floor.

If I'm being honest with you, one of my personal bad habits is leaving clothes on the floor. Between my cat's toys and my own clothes, the two of us can turn a bedroom into a disaster surprisingly quickly.

What I do to make starting more manageable is pick everything up off of the floor and set it on top of my made bed. (It's important that the bed is made so that socks and cat toys don't go missing between the sheets.) After I've cleared the floor, I like to do a quick vacuum. Then finally, piece by piece, I'll take all of the things on the bed and put them where they belong.

Finding the floor is also a great strategy for dealing with messy closets. If you try to start by folding and organizing your clothes, you can easily get bored, distracted, or discouraged along the way. But if you start by finding the floor, then your first task is easy to accomplish because it has clear parameters. We all know how stray clothes, hangers, and random items tend to get lost in the dark depths of a closet. So deal with those things first. It doesn't take long. And most importantly, the boost of satisfaction you'll feel after completing this small task will power you through the rest of the project.

No one will give you a blue ribbon for finding the floor, but you will have made progress, and that's a huge victory. Do you know how many people say they will start but never do? Well that's not you anymore! You cleared the first hurdle and now you have momentum.

Tried and True

Not all homes need a major overhaul. Some homes simply need routine decluttering, and drastic changes like the **Unlock** or **Greatest Impact** aren't necessary.

If your home only needs light work, or if you really don't know where to start, we can always resort to the **Tried and True**. These are classic and proven places to start that work for most homes.

1. Bathroom

2. Bedroom

3. Closet

4. Entryway

5. Kitchen

6. Hot Spots

Bathroom

I love starting in the bathroom because there's nothing more annoying to me than the following scenario: I open the bathroom mirror or cabinet. Things are so crowded and cluttered that something inevitably falls. The fallen item bounces around and ends up on the floor right next to the toilet. Or worse, it goes for a morning swim in the toilet.

The bathroom is where I engage in self-care, like taking a relaxing bath or following my skincare routine. This maintenance goes a long way toward balancing the stress in my life. It's also where I start and end each day as I put on makeup or prepare for bed. All of these routines are vital to my well-being so I want them to be as smooth as possible. A cluttered bathroom means guaranteed stress during all those portions of my day.

Starting my declutter here is an easy way to prioritize my health. It means that my daily rituals will continue to be as relaxing and enjoyable as possible.

Bedroom

This is where we come when our bodies need to rest. When you fall asleep at night or wake up in the morning, it's not fun to do so in the presence of a million little stressors, constantly reminding you that you need to declutter and organize.

Starting in the bedroom is another way to prioritize your health by creating a calm sleeping environment. You can wake up each day ready to work—whether that work is an office job, a parenting job, or a large-scale Space Making transformation.

Closet

Your closet is another great place to start. Clothes have a way of getting out of control quickly, and a chaotic closet can easily become a huge stress-factor in your life.

Create a sense of calm in your day and put your best foot forward as you start each morning. Wouldn't it be nice to know exactly where your clothes are, exactly when you need them?

Entryway

The entryway is the first thing you see when you walk through the door, which means it sets the tone for how you feel in your home.

It's never fun to be greeted by clutter when you come home after a long day of work. Nor is it fun to search frantically for your keys when leaving the house.

If your entryway is filled with clutter, this could be a great place for you to start so that you enter and exit your home with a calm mind.

Kitchen

The kitchen can also be a great place to start as we tend to have less emotional attachment to kitchen objects. I love to start by going through the pantry and throwing out expired items. This makes the initial declutter process simple and easy to begin.

In many homes the kitchen is a high-traffic and high-use area. Putting the kitchen in order can have a positive and stabilizing effect that ripples outward to the rest of your home.

Hot Spots

The **Hot Spots** that you took note of in your **Walk Through** are also a great place to start. You've already brought awareness to the fact that they make you feel a certain type of way, so why not kick off your Space Maker journey by knocking one out?

This can be a powerful starting point for your journey because you'll begin by transforming a **Hot Spot** into a calm spot. There was a space in your home that was bothering you and bringing anxiety into your life. Now it's gone because YOU took a stand against it! With this accomplishment you will feel:

- More in control of the clutter

- More confident in what you're capable of doing

- More motivated to keep moving forward

And that's it, five easy ways to get started!

1. The Quick Win

2. The Greatest Impact

3. The Unlock

4. Find the Floor

5. Tried and True

Choose whichever one sounds easiest and most applicable to your situation. And remember that getting started is a huge win! You've already begun to strengthen your **Declutter Muscles** and build the momentum that will keep you moving forward.

Chapter 5
Decluttering Made Simple: Sort Your Stuff Into the Easy Eight

I gave you five good options for *where to start*, now I will show you *how to start*.

First, you will start by labeling your sorting destinations. After that, you will empty the area you want to declutter and sort your items into the **Easy Eight**.

Label Your Sorting Destinations

These are the piles that you will sort your belongings into, starting with the most basic, a "keep" and a "go" pile. You may also want to add more piles such as a "try on" or "donate" or "sell" pile.

Once you have an idea of your sorting destinations, find a bin, bag, or something you can use to make it easily identifiable. Remember that we aren't buying anything just yet, so get resourceful with what you use and shop your own house for supplies. Here are some things you may already have that work well:

- reusable grocery bags

- shoe boxes

- trash bags

- cardboard boxes

- decorative baskets

- plastic containers

If the space you're working in is large enough, you could simply use different sections of the room for different piles. Just make sure that the piles don't blend into one another as they grow.

Even when you are short on sorting bins, what usually happens is that as you start decluttering you'll uncover some empty boxes or bags that you can use. In the meantime, use what you've got and adjust as you go.

For labeling these sorting piles, you can write the name on a piece of paper and tape it to the wall above the pile, or directly on to the container.

It can be tempting to skip this step and tell yourself that you don't need to label your piles. In the beginning it's probably fine. But the **During** can be chaotic and as you declutter more, your piles will grow. If these piles aren't labeled, it can be hard to keep track of what's what. This causes unnecessary stress when you're already in the midst of making difficult decisions. Trust me, later on you'll be glad you labeled your piles.

An added bonus of labeling your piles is that it helps others in your household understand your system. They may even take the initiative to add some of their own items to the "sell" or "donate" or "trash" piles. So make it easy on yourself—and everyone else—by establishing clear sorting destinations for your declutter piles.

Empty the Area You Want to Declutter

Once you've chosen a place to start and established a few sorting destinations, I want you to empty out the space you want to declutter. Empty everything... and I mean everything.

You'd be surprised by how easy it is to go wrong here. My clients always leave trash and miscellaneous items behind while claiming that the space is empty. This sort of thing happens all the time and it's comical to me.

April: "Let's empty this cabinet, basket, dresser, etc..."
Client: "OK, I did it."
April (after looking again): "There's more stuff in there!"
Client: "Oh, well that stuff doesn't count because..."

Take it all out. I mean all of it. Whatever cabinet or corner or surface you are emptying, get every last bit. Loose items, empty boxes, trash, and all!

There may be exceptions to this step like really large items that are heavy to move. But if you can't reasonably justify why something is being left there, take it out and start fresh.

Where do I put everything I've dumped out?

For now you can place it on the floor or on a countertop. Move it anywhere that will be easy for you to begin sorting it. If it's uncomfortable for you to sit on the floor, then empty everything into a bag or box that you can carry to a more convenient workstation.

For example, you could dump everything into a laundry basket and then move it next to the sofa before you start sorting. A favorite tactic of mine is to lay some towels on the bed and dump everything onto the towels. The bed is a comfortable place to sit while you sort, and it's usually isolated from the rest of the clutter—a safe and comfy sorting island.

What if there's no place to put it?

Working in small spaces can be a logistical nightmare. At times you will have no other option but to shuffle things from one room to another. It might seem like a waste of time, but it also might be the only way to complete your project.

When you feel like you're playing a real-life game of Tetris, know that you aren't doing anything wrong, you're just partaking in the **Small Space Shuffle**. It's annoying, it's normal, and it's always worth it in the end.

What if I've already decluttered that space?

Even if you don't think it needs decluttering because "it's not that bad" or "you already decluttered it last year," you should still take it all out. Many of my clients start decluttering before I arrive, but I still make them take everything out because I want them to be more meticulous. Reluctantly, and with some eye rolling, they do it.

I do this not to be annoying, but because I know they'll rethink some of their decisions as they revisit their "keep" items. I also know that their **Declutter Muscles** get stronger every time they make a pass (and by the way, this does count as a second declutter pass.)

The Importance of Touching Everything

Our homes are filled with things we've forgotten about, and by touching everything, you bring awareness to each item. Most people have never actually stopped to ask themselves how they feel about something, or why they even have it in the first place.

I want you to be intentional about everything in your home. I want you to bring awareness to every item by touching it and asking yourself, "Do I want to keep this?"

In the end, I want you to have a home full of things that you chose to be there.

Start By Sorting the Easy Eight

So you've emptied everything. You have a big pile of stuff. Now what?

I like to start with the easy and obvious decisions first. It's the best way to make a quick dent in your clutter pile and start gaining momentum. Don't let yourself get bogged down by small, tedious, or sentimental items—anything that requires too much thought.

Instead, start by looking for items that fall into one of these easily identifiable categories. I call them the **Easy Eight**.

1. Obvious Keepers

2. Trash

3. Expired Items

4. Empty Boxes

5. Duplicates

6. This Goes to a Different Room

7. Obvious Unloved Items

8. I Will Never Use That

You can have sorting piles for all of these categories and sort them all at the same time. Or if you tend to get easily overwhelmed, pick one category and focus on that one first. Once finished you can move to another category, and then another, and so on.

Easy Eight #1 Obvious Keepers

Start with the things you love. Put the obvious "Yes" items in your keep pile. This is an easy place to start and your clutter pile will immediately get smaller.

Everything that you keep should add some type of value or meaning to your life. An item can add value if it...

- makes you happy

- is a necessity for this stage of your life

- is something that makes your life easier

- reminds you of a special moment in time

- is one of the many necessities for home owners

- benefits your health and well being

- is a daily essential item

- is something you use to entertain guests

Remember, the whole point of Space Making is to give these items the space and ability to shine. These are the things that make you happy. We want them to be easy to find, easy to display, easy to use.

In order to do that, we need to thin down the rest of your clutter.

Easy Eight #2 Trash

This is another quick way to make progress. It's pretty easy to start by pulling out all of the trash. That could be old newspapers, old receipts, socks with holes in them, printed MapQuest directions from the 90s, broken or unusable items, you name it.

Chaos breeds chaos and trash has a way of accumulating in those piles that need to be decluttered.

Easy Eight #3 Expired Items

This category is a great way to make progress and it works well for food, beauty, medical, and even some home maintenance items.

Find expired products in your refrigerator, spice cabinet, bathroom drawers, pantry, junk box, medical supplies, or whatever area you're starting in. Most of these items should have a written expiration date on the label, though sometimes it can be hard to locate. If the product has a "use by" date, there should be a symbol of a jar with a number inside followed by an "M." For example: 6M, 12M, 24M. This indicates how many months the product is good for after opening.

Medicine and first aid supplies tend to expire fairly quickly and you can count on the expiration dates being easily visible on each product. You can even check your adhesive bandages which tend to get gooey when past their prime.

Unfortunately not all products have a printed expiration date, which means you'll need to inspect the product for yourself. Does it pass the sniff test? In the future, for the containers without dates, a quick fix is to jot down the date you open them. Write it on the label, the lid, or the container itself. This way you won't need to question whether or not a product is still safe to use because you'll have a written record.

Here are two important things to keep in mind as you sort your expired items.

First, although an item may technically be good for years past the expiration date (like spices), if it's been in your cabinet for the past 5 years then you have to ask yourself, "Am I really going to use this?" Most likely, if something has remained unused all those years, then all it's doing is taking up valuable space.

Second, if you come across items that recently expired or are about to expire (especially food and beauty items), set them in a new location for a **Use it or Lose it Challenge.** I like to group and place these items where they are most visible. This could be on the countertop, in a designated bag or bin, or even on a labeled shelf in the refrigerator. Put them somewhere where you'll have to notice them. You'll have to see them every day, challenging you to either use them soon or part with them.

Easy Eight #4 Empty Boxes

This one deserves a category all to itself. Empty boxes have a strange way of hanging around because they pose as something you "might need later." I see this repeatedly in my clients' homes. It's some sort of clutter phenomenon because everyone swears that there is something inside all the boxes, but when we open them they're always empty.

There are a million ways to justify keeping your empty boxes, but when was the last time you really needed the box that your iphone or hair dryer came in? What's more important to you, that empty box, or using that space for something more valuable to you?

For the packaging that comes from expensive tech items like computers and phones, I like to keep them until I've passed the return or exchange period. After that I recycle the boxes or repurpose them as organizers in my home.

Removing empty boxes is a quick and easy way to create some valuable space in your home.

***

Bonus Tip: Calm the Chaos

I told you that things are going to get worse before they get better. But no matter how well prepared you are, there will always come a time when the mess threatens to overwhelm you.

When the work of decluttering is redlining out of control, take a moment to calm the chaos.

This can be done in a few different ways. You can...

- *Straighten your decluttering piles*

- *Rearrange your piles so that it's easier to move through the room*

> - *Make sure that your sorting destinations are not blending into one another*
>
> - *Take out the trash*
>
> - *Move the donation items to a "staging area" like the garage or patio, or load them straight into the car*
>
> - *Open a window, turn off the loud music, give a treat to the meowing cat (I mean you, Izzy!)*
>
> - *Do anything that brings order to the decluttering environment and lowers the level of overwhelm*
>
> *Afterward, you'll feel a greater sense of calm and clarity about your project and you'll be able to move forward.*

Easy Eight #5 Duplicates

When you're unorganized, it's easy to forget what you have and accidentally purchase duplicates. Bathrooms, kitchens and closets tend to be a breeding ground for such items.

You can easily eliminate some duplicate items by comparing them to their counterparts. Has one expired? Is one in better shape than the other? If so, keep the nicer one and declutter the other. For some things like food spices or shampoo bottles, you may be able to merge a couple of half-used items into a single container.

And then there will be some duplicates that you will want to keep, like extra mascara or toothpaste. This is fine and perfectly practical. Especially if it's something that you will eventually need to repurchase, there's no sense in decluttering it.

For now I recommend collecting your duplicates in one place, whether it's a shoe box, a bag, a basket, or a shelf in the cabinet. Be sure to label it clearly so that you don't forget about it, but don't worry about perfect organization right now because that will distract you from decluttering. As you continue your declutter you will likely add more duplicates to this area. When we get to the **After**, you can create a permanent **Department** for your back stock. Then you can shop your personal **Department** store before having to go somewhere else!

Easy Eight #6 This Goes To A Different Room

Identify the items that don't belong in the current space you're working in and take them back where they belong. If you don't have a permanent home for them already, no problem. Just deliver them to where you think they will go.

For example, if you find clothing in your office, take it to the closet it belongs in. If you find plastic food containers in the garage, take them back to the kitchen. You don't need to be too precise in this process. I don't want you to start reorganizing or start decluttering the kitchen when you return the plastic containers. Just leave them in their new home or somewhere in the vicinity.

This act of returning items might make you feel like you're only making things worse. It can be hard to not let yourself get lured into starting a side project, but this is when you need to be mentally tough and focus on finishing one project at a time. Even if that means that another space is getting messy in the meantime, it's all part of the process and you promised me that you would trust the process. So ignore all other messy areas except for the one you are working in at the moment. This will help you work quickly and efficiently.

Things may get a little disorderly as you continue through the declutter, but that's perfectly normal and it's one reason why we do **Multiple Passes**.

Easy Eight #7 Obvious Unloved Items

Identify and declutter all those things that don't leave you feeling excited for the next season of your life.

This is especially applicable to closets because it's easy to identify how a certain piece of clothing makes you feel. If you have pants that squeeze you a little too much and make you feel self conscious, get them out. If you have clothing from an old job that is filled with bad memories, out!

I want you to make space for the things in your life that you love. Your space is too precious for anything that you obviously don't love.

Easy Eight #8 I Will Never Use That

This category requires brutal honesty. If there are obvious items that you aren't going to ever use again, take them out.

These may include, but are not limited to: pantry items, kitchen gadgets, clothing, home decor, hand bags, and craft supplies.

These items can be a little harder to identify than the items in the previous categories. They might not be immediately obvious, but try to be honest with yourself. What would your future self say if you asked them, "Will I ever use this?"

Getting these things out of the way in the beginning will not only create more physical space, it will free up mental space for you to focus on more pressing areas of your declutter.

That's the **Easy Eight**! When you're staring at a big pile of clutter and wondering where to begin, these eight categories will help you make quick progress and see exciting results in no time.

Bonus Tip: How to Declutter with Friends & Family

I always say that you can't force someone to declutter. If you try, it will likely result in a fight. So how do you effectively declutter when your stuff is mixed with someone else's stuff?

Let's look at two very common scenarios:

    1. *Decluttering in a Shared Space*

    2. *Helping a Family Member*

Scenario #1 - Decluttering in a Shared Space

This can be one of the most challenging aspects of a declutter, especially if you and your roommate/partner/family members have different ideas of what it means to "live with less."

Here are a few ideas to help you navigate the reality of decluttering in a shared space.

Don't declutter what doesn't belong to you

It's a simple rule that we learned as kids, "If it's not yours, don't touch it." How would you like it if your significant other took the liberty to donate your clothes without asking? Not great, right?

No matter how well-intentioned you may be, we're all on our own journey and it's best to let others arrive at their decisions in their own time. Let the owner decide the fate of their own belongings.

Ignore it

On the surface this sounds childish, but I'd argue that it's actually the most mature route to take.

Control what you can control. Even if that means putting blinders on and pretending that you don't see the other person's clutter, do it. Declutter around their belongings.

With permission, box it up

Sometimes it makes sense for you to put away someone else's clutter until they're ready to sort through it.

I do this often for my clients whose partners don't have time to declutter at the same time we're working, or for those who aren't ready to declutter. With their permission, we gather their items and place them in storage bins as we declutter each new area. Then when they have time and feel ready, they can sort through *their boxes.*

Keep in mind this requires clear and ongoing communication. Together you'll need to discuss which items are acceptable to store away, where those items will be stored, and who exactly is responsible for labeling and storing them.

For the willing, but hesitant

For someone that is willing to declutter but is feeling hesitant or intimidated by the idea, try giving them a super-small-sized **Quick Win**. *Transfer some of their items to a shoe box (or something of a similar size) and ask if they can sort through it.*

Handing over a laundry basket full of clutter may overwhelm them, so keep it small. Give them a manageable task so that they get their **Quick Win** *and all the accompanying benefits.*

Lead by example

Actions speak louder than words, so work on your clutter first. As you experience the transformation in your life and home, they will notice. They will see the physical change in the home and they will see how you've changed.

Maybe your self-improvement efforts will inspire the ones you live with. Maybe not. But you certainly won't inspire them by trying to force them or drag them into it before they are ready. So focus your energy on what you can control and lead by example.

Move your stuff

By this I mean to literally separate your belongings by moving them somewhere else. While not always ideal, separating your things will allow you to focus completely on your designated area. You won't have to look at their clutter anymore because you'll no longer share the space. If you can each have your own space then you'll both be able to do as you please and not stress the other out.

For example, if a messy closet is the problem, is there somewhere else in your home that you can move your clothes (or their clothes) so that you no longer share the same closet? Is there any way to do it? Maybe you don't have space right now, but over the course of your declutter project you could make it a priority to free up a new closet space.

A lot of families have suboptimal systems or setups they've been using for years or even decades. No one ever thinks to question the arrangement because it's "always been that way."

Simple moves like separating a closet space have been known to save a marriage or two for my clients (their words, not mine). They are that powerful.

Scenario #2 - Helping a Family Member

I've spent years helping family members and loved ones declutter and organize their homes. And while the results have been rewarding, the road to progress was challenging, with fights, tears and stress along the way.

For those of you that set out to help your family, I want to share some takeaways and lessons that I learned from my own experience. My hope is that the process can be as smooth as possible for everyone involved and you can even have some family fun along the way.

Here are some things to keep in mind as you work together:

It's not about you

As you're decluttering, keep in mind that this process is not about how much stuff you think your family member should have in their home because this isn't about you, it's about them.

This is something that sounds like a no-brainer, but I've found that when it comes to friends and family, it's easy to cross the line from time to time. As you're helping them, it can be easy to pressure them into adopting your same beliefs on how much stuff a person should have.

Ultimately, we all need to decide for ourselves how much stuff we feel comfortable owning and maintaining. As for you? Think of yourself as a guide and cheerleader who gives tips and encouragement, not a doctor who gives orders and prescriptions. Be a helpful guide as they discover their new level of comfort in owning less.

You'll need even more patience & understanding than you think

Decluttering with younger or older family members can be difficult because every generation was raised under different circumstances with different beliefs. When you feel yourself getting frustrated, try to put yourself in their shoes and remember that there will always be things that you just can't relate to.

Practicing more patience and trying to be as understanding as possible will make the process better for everyone.

One other somber reminder I want to share is that especially as your grandparents and parents get older, they will likely be coping with the loss of their parents, friends, and loved ones. There are countless ways these feelings and memories can surface as you declutter. If you're going to err one way or another, err on the side of being gentle.

Don't skip the Walk Through

*Just because they are family and you think you know them, don't skip the **Walk Through**. (See the **Walk Through** chapter in the **Before** if you missed it.)*

Go through the space with them, listening and asking questions along the way to help you better understand how they interact in their space and with their stuff. Never assume, just ask.

The Last Resort

I hope that by implementing the information in this book, you'll set yourself up for success as you declutter. But family dynamics can be complicated and decluttering together can complicate things even further.

Don't let things get so bad that you storm out or damage your relationship. If you feel like things are escalating to that point, take some time away from the project to clear your head. Try to identify what's going wrong and practice good communication skills when conveying this to your loved one. You may be able to talk about it rationally so that you find a solution that keeps you pushing forward. But if you feel like tensions are rising to a point that's unhealthy for your relationship, it may be time to walk away from the declutter.

I hope that you finish the projects you start, but never at the risk of losing your loved ones. If there is no seeing eye-to-eye, tell them that you won't be able to finish the project and brainstorm what a good stopping point would be for the both of you. Keep the most important thing the most important thing.

Chapter 6
Focus Your Attention to Build Unstoppable Momentum

If you want to be as efficient as possible, your only focus should be on decluttering.

An easy way to get side tracked is thinking too many steps ahead. Your mind starts time traveling, thinking of all the options for re-organizing your cabinets or about the new bookshelves you can buy for better storage. You're wondering how you'll decorate the living room or how you'll coordinate a garage sale before you're even done decluttering.

The **During** is already difficult. Why cause yourself more stress by overloading your brain with these thoughts? What I see with my clients is that 99% of these side-thoughts and worries naturally work themselves out over the course of the declutter.

Efficiency is related to focus. You know that in the **During** you should only be decluttering, so it's a question of how well you can keep your focus. Not only will you move faster through the declutter if you stay focused, you'll also make sharper decisions about what to keep and let go.

Declutter One Area at a Time

There's a lot of debate in the decluttering/organizing community about this question: What's the best way to proceed through your decluttering effort?

Some experts say you should declutter your home category by category. Start with clothes and declutter all the clothes. Tomorrow, do all of your books, and so on. I'm not a fan of decluttering by categories because I think it's impractical and mentally draining.

When you skip from room to room while focusing on a single category, you rarely get the mental satisfaction of a victory. The danger of getting distracted grows as you move from room to room. The longer a category takes you to declutter, the easier it is to start feeling frustrated.

I much prefer to focus my efforts on one area at a time, regardless of the category. I like decluttering from room to room, or if an entire room is too daunting, breaking it down even smaller and going area by area within a room. It's more rewarding to tackle do-able areas because you get to enjoy lots of little victories throughout the day (as opposed to spending a whole day or even multiple days on a single category).

So if it feels too daunting to try and tackle all of your clothes at once (or any other category for that matter), don't worry! All you need to do is start small. Pick a room, an area, or a single pile and declutter it until you're done.

When you finish one task at a time before moving to the next, you begin to create a sense of order amidst the chaos.

Quick Wins: Your Secret Weapon to Stay Efficient and Build Confidence

I use this approach for all of my clients who are overwhelmed with their clutter. But it works especially well for my clients with ADHD because it gives them well-defined goals that can be done in a short amount of time, so it helps us stay focused.

Quick Wins are not just useful at the very beginning of a project, they are useful anytime you're feeling distracted or overwhelmed and need to focus.

For example, if the bedroom clutter is causing your head to spin, make a **Quick Win** of the pile on the dresser. I'm a fan of moving the clutter and sorting in another room because as soon as you move the clutter, you immediately get to experience how calm the top of the dresser looks and feels when it's clutter free. You don't even have to declutter anything to experience that first glimmer of hope and change! It feels so good to see that smooth dresser surface. How long has it been since you've seen it? Ride the wave of those good vibes as you sort through your pile in a different location.

If tackling a full pile feels too stressful, dump some of the clutter into a shoe box and take it to the living room to sort. The smaller the task, the easier it is to keep your focus and finish that task.

When the shoebox is empty you'll feel great. Maybe you'll go and fill another shoebox to sort. With each victory you will feel more and more confident in what you're capable of. You may even trick yourself into decluttering your whole house!

***

Story Time

One time a potential client sent me a video tour of her home. I was heartbroken as I watched her walk from room to room and describe the state of her home. The heartbreaking part was not the amount of stuff, but the sound of defeat in her voice.

Her 2-bedroom apartment was completely maxed out with clothes and clutter, but I could see how much potential it had. I couldn't wait to get started.

Each morning our work day started with coffee and a chat. (I love starting a day of decluttering with a coffee date because it not only lightens the mood, but it gives me time to learn more about the person I'm helping.) This is my favorite kind of girl talk, **Coffee and Clutter***. During our first chat she told me that she felt like she was drowning. She said she'd been ready to declutter for quite some time, but she was too overwhelmed by everything and didn't know where to start.*

> *Knowing that we had our work cut out for us, I wanted to start small on the first day. I wanted her to declutter just enough to start strengthening her **Declutter Muscles**, but not so much that she'd feel exhausted or defeated.*
>
> *I explained to her the idea of **Quick Wins** and we started by clearing the mini pile of clothing and clutter that was sitting on her blanket chest near the entryway to her bedroom. It was a short project that took less than 30 minutes, but the results were powerful.*
>
> *Within 30 minutes of officially starting her Space Making journey, she was able to see and feel the results of her newly cleared surface. I believe her exact words as she stared at the space were, "I feel like I can breathe easier."*
>
> *Throughout that first day, we tackled **Quick Win** after **Quick Win** in the 3 hours we spent decluttering together. And I swear to you that by the end of that day, she didn't need my help anymore. She was a completely different person in the face of her clutter. In 3 hours she went from feeling defeated to wildly confident, and it's all thanks to the power of **Quick Wins**.*

Speed Decluttering: How to Trick Yourself Into Decluttering Quickly

Speed decluttering is a simple tool you can use to help you focus and make fast progress. Set a timer and race to get a project done before the timer goes off.

You want a time that is not too long, but not too short. If it's too long you'll burn out. If it's too short, it's unrealistic and you set yourself up for failure. The sweet spot tends to be around 15-20 minutes or so.

If you come to something that's going to distract you, like a tedious task or a box of sentimental items, set it aside for now. These types of items deserve more time and don't make sense for speed decluttering.

While you can integrate speed decluttering into any project, here are the two main ways I like to use this tool.

#1 Small Tasks

Smaller projects are a perfect match for speed decluttering. It could be a small area or a single category that you focus on as you race to finish it in the allotted time.

Categories you may consider for this are shoes, spices, makeup, a purse, or a basket of toys. Small areas that may work well for you could be a small closet, a kitchen drawer, a cabinet, or a bookshelf. Really any small decluttering task on your to do list that you're procrastinating would be great for incorporating this technique.

One of my clients successfully decluttered her bathroom this way. It was a smaller project consisting of two areas: the shower and storage behind the mirror, perfect for a small task. We set the timer for 15 minutes and raced against the clock to declutter the two areas before the timer finished. Even though the act of decluttering was stressful to her, speed decluttering became her superpower and we used this technique in other areas of her home as well.

#2 Large Tasks

For larger projects, you can set a timer for 10-20 minutes and do as much as you can during that time. After the timer goes off simply reset it and race again. Continue resetting the timer until you finish the task at hand. I like to think of larger projects as entire rooms like the garage, bedroom, living room, kitchen, etc.

Speed decluttering closets is particularly popular among my clients. Though a closet is a small area, it tends to have a large volume of items that can feel rather daunting to sort through. To help us feel less overwhelmed by the sheer scale of the items we need to process, we'll set a timer and race to do as much as we can before the timer goes off. When it does go off, we'll take a short water break and then set a new timer and get back to it. We continue to repeat this process until we've finished the entire closet.

Speed decluttering works for two reasons. First of all, it takes large, dreadful projects and disguises them as little, do-able, mini-tasks. Secondly, the pressure of the clock gives you razor sharp focus. You simply have no time to think about how much you hate decluttering, what you're going to do with all the stuff, or how guilty or embarrassed you might feel. Because you're focused, you'll work quicker. When you work quicker, you'll make more progress. And when you see that progress, you'll feel more motivated!

Speed decluttering is an amazing way to switch your attitude from, "I can't do this" to "I can do this!"

***

> ## Bonus Tip: Trust the Process
>
> *Space Making is a marathon and it can be easy to lose sight of the goal when you're in the thick of it, especially as your home gets messier in the process. The **During** isn't pretty and that's why you don't see it on TV. But this whole, "getting worse before it gets better" thing is normal.*
>
> *When you're in the **Messy Middle** and can't see the finish line, I want you to adopt this mantra, "Trust the process."*
>
> *Repeat it to yourself like a broken record, "Trust the process. Trust the process. Trust the process. Trust the process."*
>
> *Everything you are going through is a normal part of the process and in order to get to the other side you have to keep pushing forward. It doesn't matter how big or small the progress is, progress is progress. It counts!*
>
> *Focus on finishing one task at a time. Become your own cheerleader and celebrate your progress. If you clear out a basket of stuff, "Yahoo!" High five yourself. Do a happy dance. Be your own hype person.*
>
> *Trust the process, it will all be worth it in the end.*

Chapter 7
Mindfully Process Your Belongings for the Benefit of Yourself & Others

After you sort your items, they need to go somewhere. Will they go to the donation center or back into your closet? What about the maybes and the 'just in case' items? In this chapter, we'll discuss what to do with the stuff you declutter.

Let's start with the most obvious category first: your keepers. What should you do with the things you're keeping?

Roughly Organize Your Keepers into Departments

Try to put the items you want to keep in the most logical place. Put the clothes you want to keep back in the closet, and the food items back in the cabinet. Try to put things where they belong, or at least group like items together. You can think of these groupings as **Departments**.

Keep in mind that the broader you keep these **Departments**, the less overwhelming it will be. Instead of grouping all of your shirts by color (overwhelming), simply group all clothes together in the "Closet Department". Don't get hyper fixated on the groupings. At that point you really are getting distracted from decluttering. Instead, stick to **Rough Organization**. (Also remember that the **Buy Ban** is still in effect, so make use of whatever temporary organizer you can find around your home!)

This may mean collecting light bulbs, tape, scissors and batteries, and putting them in a shopping bag that serves as your temporary "Miscellaneous Home Things Department." You could use a big cardboard box to hold all of your sandals and summer shoes. Or you could gather all stamps, envelopes, paperclips, pens, and stationery items into an empty container that now becomes the "Stationery Department".

If you don't know where something goes, just set it to the side for now. I like to designate a bin or box specifically for those items that I don't know what to do with. This is the "Don't Know Department." The most important thing to remember in these moments is not to get hung up on indecision. Instead, accept and expect that you won't have a home for everything right away, and that's okay!

It will get easier to sort things into their proper **Departments** as you go along. Your home will feel less chaotic throughout the decluttering process, and you will set yourself up for success on your next pass of decluttering.

Just in Case Items

Unpopular opinion, but I'm a proponent of keeping those 'just in case' items that many decluttering experts tell you to let go of.

What I mean by a 'just in case' item is anything you think you might need down the road, within reason. It could be those shoes that you haven't worn in a year, but you do use them for fancy events on occasion. It could be the extra makeup foundation that you aren't quite sure about yet or some unread books sitting on your shelf. There are millions of 'just in case' scenarios that could fall into this category and contrary to popular advice, I think you should be cautious before decluttering these items.

If this is your first pass of decluttering, it can be easy to get excited about the idea of living with less. You might get so excited that you rage through your home like a decluttering storm, throwing away anything that isn't nailed down. But over-decluttering to the point of regret isn't a sustainable approach. Nor is repurchasing items that you'll end up needing later. I really don't like the idea that if an item is cheap, you should just throw it away and plan to re-buy it later if needed.

I'm no poster child for sustainability, but I do believe that we have a responsibility to take care of our planet. With the amount of waste we're already producing through our decluttering, the least we can do is proceed with a little caution if we think an item may be of use to us later on.

Holding on to some extra items doesn't necessarily mean you'll keep them forever. The reality of **Multiple Passes** allows us to give ourselves a little grace. If ultimately you decide that you will never realistically need the item again, declutter it! It's really not a big deal to declutter something at a later time. What's more important is that you declutter confidently with a long-term mindset.

This is the mindful art of Space Making. I want you to focus on sustainability—not just for the planet—but for the longevity of your decluttering decisions.

Of course this isn't a free pass to keep everything! If you let 'just in case' be your excuse to hold on to more than you need, you'll only impede your progress. It's a balance to learn how many of these types of items to keep and how many to let go of, but with experimentation and routine maintenance you'll find the best equilibrium for your household.

Home Decor & Organizers

Home decor and organizers are two of the most common 'just in case' items that I find in a declutter. It's hard to make snap judgements about these items because they are related to the **After**, but you're still in the **During**.

In all my declutters we designate a specific area to gather all the organizers and home decor pieces we uncover. If you like a decor piece but you don't know where it should go, just keep it for now. And you never know when an organizer will come in handy, so keep it for now, just in case. What you're doing is building a stockpile to pull from at a later time.

Opinions on home decor shift rapidly as a home gets decluttered. It's impossible to see in the beginning, but later your home will feel like a blank slate. You'll view your items and spaces in a completely new light.

Once you make it to the **After**, you'll have a readily available stockpile of organizers and home decor pieces that you can choose from! Rather than run to the store, you can first shop your own home using those pieces you kept while decluttering.

Then, when your home is organized and decorated to your liking, you can take whatever you didn't use to the donation center. Easy!

Maybes

When you come across something that you can't make a firm decision on, place it in a maybe pile to revisit later. This is another category that you can establish with your sorting destinations.

Some people think that having a maybe pile is cheating the process, but I strongly disagree, and here's why.

When you declutter I want you to declutter with confidence. I don't want you to regret or rebuy the items because you decluttered them hastily. I would rather you wait out your thought process until you can come to a firm resolution, even if it takes a little longer and those items occupy space in the meantime.

What I also see happen with clients is that while they continue decluttering they subconsciously process their feelings regarding whatever they put in the maybe pile. They might be reasoning with themselves about the reality of actually using the item again, or working through some of the emotional attachments they discovered it has, but the mental process continues happening in the background as they keep decluttering. All of this thinking time is a necessary part of the Space Making process.

For women especially, our bodies change throughout the month and those changes can affect how our clothes make us feel. Some months my pants fit me better than others. It happens. Because I'm anticipating these changes, instead of decluttering something right away, I might put it in my maybe pile. From there I can think about it and make a sounder decision later on. After all, I already own it, so I'd rather take more time before I permanently remove it from my closet.

As you sort through your clothing, you can also set aside a maybe pile for all the pieces you aren't sure fit you. Or for pieces that you aren't sure suit your style anymore. Set them aside and have a big try-on day where you address all of these items.

Though it might not look like it, having a maybe pile is progress. It's a way of saying, "I don't feel confident enough to get rid of this completely, but I'm still not sure if I want to keep it. I will decide on it in the next pass."

Eliminate the anxiety about making the wrong decision and revisit the pile later. This will allow you to get back to your quick and focused decluttering efforts. And with more time, you will be able to process your thoughts and make confident decisions about your maybes.

Sensitive Items

If you aren't ready to declutter something, don't force it!

Sorting through difficult emotions takes time. It's easy to overwhelm yourself if you feel you have to decide in the moment. Release yourself from that pressure.

It's okay to wait on something until you feel ready to make a decision. There is no rush. Especially when it comes to navigating grief and trauma, it's going to take time. At the end of the day this is your declutter journey, no one else's. Make the best decision for you when the time is right.

***

Story Time

On the first pass of decluttering that I helped my Mom with, there was a bookshelf in the corner collecting dust and clutter. It wasn't functioning well for her. If we could have removed it, we could have created space to move the furniture around and open up the small bedroom.

When I asked my mom about it, her response was a firm "No." After talking with her more about it I learned that it was my Nana's who had recently passed. She knew it wasn't functioning well in the space, but she wasn't ready to let it go just yet. So we decided to keep it and relocate it to a different room where it would function better for her.

When I came back 6 months later for another pass of decluttering I was hesitant to bring up the bookshelf again. But you know what? I didn't have to because she brought it up on her own. As we were working she said, "I'm ready to say goodbye to the bookshelf."

What happened in those 6 months is that she gave herself the time and space she needed to think about it and then when she felt ready she was able to make a decision.

With so many emotions attached to our belongings, sometimes you'll need a longer period of time to feel it out. Don't force yourself to let go of something before you're ready. If you do, you may regret it. Instead, wait it out. Make the final call when you feel it's time.

Sell Piles

It can be tempting to want to sell everything that you declutter to recover some of the money you originally spent. And while I understand this logic, I don't think this is always the best course of action.

While I fully support selling what you can at a consignment store, garage sale, or via an online platform if you have the space, selling things takes a lot of time and energy. In the meantime, these piles will continue taking up valuable space in your home until you get around to selling them (if you ever do).

I don't want to discourage anyone from earning some extra cash, but I do want to be honest about the logistics of selling and I want to ask you, "Is it more valuable for you to earn some extra cash or is it more valuable for you to remove the clutter from your house immediately?" There isn't a right or wrong answer. For some, that extra money is worth it; for others the free space is more valuable.

No matter what you choose, I want you to be honest with yourself about the work and additional time that selling will require, on top of the time and effort you're already putting into your declutter.

All things considered, which is more valuable for your current situation - selling or donating?

Donate Piles

I find a lot of items in donation piles that honestly should not be there. While every donation center has different requirements, be responsible and donate with dignity.

I've found that most of the time, we're inclined to put as much as we can into our donation piles because it makes us feel better about how much we're decluttering. It helps us feel less guilty for all the money we spent (and maybe wasted), and less upset about how much of our stuff is headed straight for the landfill. When we add things to our donation piles we think, "Even though I don't want this anymore, it can go to a new home where someone else will love it." That can be true, but one man's trash is not *always* another man's treasure. Sometimes it's just trash.

As you declutter, donate with dignity by ensuring that what you donate is free of stains, holes, rust, tears, and general damage. Is it usable? Is it in working condition at least? Do you think it can truly be valuable to someone or are you just trying to ease your own guilt?

Because every donation center has different policies for what they'll accept, it's a good idea to call beforehand and get a list of what they'll take. You can also check with your local shelters (for animals too) to get a list of what they'll take. You may find that a shelter will accept more than your local donation center will.

Re-Gifting Items

The same can be said of re-gifting items to friends or family. It's easy to assume that a loved one would want whatever you declutter. It can even make you feel better about what you decluttered because it's going to the home of a loved one. While this can be true, it's not always the case.

Before you give, ask the recipient if they'd like to have it and if they have room for it. Give them an opportunity to respond honestly. This way you can give your loved ones things they really want instead of burdening them with things they don't.

Recycling

Just because everything can't be donated doesn't mean that the alternative is the trash. There are plenty of resources available both locally and online for items that can't be donated, like unrepairable clothing, shoes and electronics. These options will help keep more of what you declutter out of the landfill.

Check your city's recycling requirements to see what types of materials they accept. Many chain hardware stores often recycle light bulbs and batteries while electronic stores will often accept old TVs, computers, cellphones, printer ink and more.

Chapter 8

How to Navigate Difficult Emotions & Keep Moving Forward

There's no way to declutter without navigating some difficult emotions along the way. That's why I call it **Declutter Therapy**. Guilt and Embarrassment. Shame and Sorrow. We all experience these feelings at some point or another. You are not alone.

But you do have a choice to make. You can let these feelings hold you back and keep you stuck in the past, or you can let them propel you into the future. Let's talk about what to do when these fears and anxieties arise.

Money Guilt

It's easy to look at your declutter pile and see dollar signs. You might feel guilty for all the money spent and perhaps wasted over the years. As uncomfortable as these feelings are, the only way through it is through it. The way I see it is that you can continue holding onto the guilt and let it hold you back, or you can forgive yourself and move forward.

What a Space Maker considers is not the monetary value of an item, but the value it adds to their life. This is a great time to reflect on your **Compass Question**. Do you love this item and want to make space for it in your home? Or are you simply keeping it because you feel guilty letting it go?

If you're ready to let it go, thank the item for the value it brought to your life and say goodbye.

Finally, try to use money guilt as motivation as you move forward in your Space Maker journey. The next time you're out shopping, remember those feelings because the time to think about the lifespan of an item is not after purchasing but before. When you're about to make that next impulse buy, ask yourself, "Is this going to end up in my declutter pile in a year?"

This is your life, make it great! Spend it in a home that you love, surrounded by the things you love, not by things that make you feel guilty.

Gift Guilt

As we talk about gift guilt I'm going to assume that no one who feels this way is ungrateful or trying to be an a-hole. The reason you have guilt in the first place is because you're a thoughtful person who's conscious of a loved one's feelings. But gift guilt is a very real emotion, crippling many homes around the world, so let's talk about it.

First of all, if you have a sentimental gift that you feel guilty about letting go of, remember that there is no pressure to let it go right this minute. Wait a while. Allow yourself to process your emotions and strengthen your **Declutter Muscles**. This is your declutter journey, after all. Go at your own pace. When (and if) you're ready, you can let it go.

But for gift guilt items with less sentimental attachment, let's revisit Rule #2: No **Shoulding**.

April: (holding up dress that doesn't resemble client's personality) "Is this something that you'd like to keep?"

Client: "Well... it doesn't really fit me and I don't really think it's my color."

April: "Do you ever wear it?"

Client: "No. But...I need to keep it."

April: "Why do you need to keep it?"

Client: "Well I should keep it because my Mom gave it to me. I don't want to hurt her feelings."

I don't want you to base your decisions on what you think you should be doing. I want you to base them on what you want. If you really are keeping something out of guilt, what's the point? Is your loved one going to be really upset that you didn't keep their gift? Do they even remember that they gave it to you?

Most often your family and friends just want you to be happy and healthy. If the clutter in your home is bringing unnecessary stress and anxiety into your home, don't you think that they would be a cheerleader for you as you make whatever changes you deem necessary?

Don't let guilt prevent you from living the life you want. Say a thank you to that item and place it in your donation bin with gratitude and appreciation for the person who gave it to you.

Embarrassment & Shame

At some point you may feel embarrassed or ashamed at how bad things have gotten, how much money you've lost, how messy your home has become, how precious memories got lost or ruined by the clutter. These are normal emotions that almost everyone has at some point while decluttering.

As Space Makers we're not going to let these feelings overwhelm us. Instead, let's use them as a tool to move forward. When these feelings do arise, allow yourself to acknowledge and embrace them. But don't allow yourself to linger so long that you get lost and lose sight of your Space Making efforts.

What's important in this moment is that you are choosing to move forward. When you began this journey you said, "Enough is enough!" You declared that you want your home to change. So forgive yourself and focus on moving forward because what waits for you on the other side of the embarrassment and clutter is something better than you could ever imagine.

It's more space for what you love. Space to have family gatherings. Space to cook for loved ones. Space to craft and build and create. Space to breathe.

That's something to be proud of and excited about!

***

Bonus Tip: Don't Sleep Where You Declutter

Decluttering is mentally and physically exhausting. You need to give yourself time to recharge and relax in between your declutter sessions. This will help you make sound decisions and have the mental and physical capacity to finish what you start. Your brain needs to remove itself entirely from decluttering at the end of the night and that can be challenging to do if you're sleeping where you declutter. Your clutter may even show up in your dreams! I'm not joking about this.

If you're able to, at the end of the night, shut the door on the clutter and unwind. If this isn't possible, try creating a calm zone somewhere around your house that you can escape to when you need to shut down your brain.

If your bedroom is full of clutter, you might consider making it the first room you declutter. This way at least you'll have a calm space to rest for the remainder of your project.

This is something that is so easily overlooked, but truly has the power to make or break your project. Give yourself a break, don't sleep where you declutter.

Chapter 9
How to Know When You've Decluttered Enough

It's completely normal to finish your first round of decluttering and feel like you want (or need) to do more.

The good news is that, of all the decluttering passes, the first tends to be the biggest and most chaotic while the following passes get progressively easier. This is because with each pass you have less stuff and your **Declutter Muscles** are stronger.

The Magic of Multiple Passes and Why Rough Organization Really Works

The magic of **Multiple Passes** is that, as you get more organized and do a better job of grouping like items together, decluttering becomes easier and easier.

It's hard to declutter effectively at the beginning of your Space Making journey when your home is in a state of chaos. How can you make a final decision on sweaters when you keep finding new ones in surprising locations? How can you assess your holiday decor when there are six boxes scattered across three different rooms?

Half the battle of that first big pass of decluttering is getting "organized enough" so that you can actually begin to take stock of each category.

On your second pass, it'll be easier to see what you have and easier to declutter more items. On the third pass you'll make even more confident decisions.

The amount of passes you make through your home and/or categories will be up to you. If you're starting with a ton of stuff, more passes may be necessary until you feel confident with what you have left. The most important gauge for how many passes you will need is how you feel about the area in question. If your living room feels calm and under control, don't waste your time with another pass. But if, say, your closet is still stressing you out, do a quick declutter and re-organization. Keep doing it again and again until you find yourself saying, "I feel good about this now."

The flow of **Multiple Passes** is like a see-saw between decluttering and organizing. With each pass you'll get more organized and you'll be able to make stronger decisions. Eventually you will reach a point where you feel fully satisfied with the things you have left and the organizing systems you've built around them.

Balancing Comfort and Discomfort as You Work Through Multiple Passes

Space Making is a balancing act. There are times when you need to be compassionate and understanding with yourself, but there are also times when compassion can masquerade as an excuse.

I don't want you to mistake the compassionate approach for a free pass to keep everything.

Sometimes you'll need to push yourself out of your comfort zone and let go of things that are no longer serving a purpose in your home. In fact, these things are actually weighing you down and if you let go of them you will feel so much lighter!

The less you push yourself into discomfort, the longer you will keep yourself from stepping into your new life. If you find yourself keeping more than you would like, experiment with pushing yourself to let go of something (or a few somethings) that you're holding onto. How does it feel to let it go? Was it as horrible as you thought? Do you regret it?

Another great benefit to doing **Multiple Passes** is that you give yourself time to process your feelings and emotions. It's very common for my clients to let go of more maybe items and sentimental/emotionally charged items during later passes.

I've noticed that a lot of my clients benefit from waiting a few months between passes. Taking a break allows you to rest physically, but it also gives you time to process all of the changes that resulted from the previous round. It's quiet thinking time and you likely won't even realize that you're thinking about it, but it does take time to sort through how you feel.

As you progress in your journey, keep experimenting with finding your perfect balance between showing yourself compassion and pushing yourself outside your comfort zone. Remember that it's never just one or the other. You'll need both if you want to reach your **After**.

How Much Stuff Do You Really Need?

"No one needs that many clothes."

"No one needs so many books."

"No one needs all those shoes."

I often see these comments under my decluttering videos on YouTube implying that the Space Maker in training needs to declutter more aggressively.

It's funny to me how quickly these commenters can judge a stranger's life and assume they know what's best for someone else. These comments usually come from new or casual viewers who aren't familiar with the Space Maker community. In contrast, the core Space Maker community is a lot slower to judge. They are much more likely to respond with words of compassion and encouragement, celebrating all progress no matter how big or small.

That's because for a Space Maker, there is no set rule for how many things you should or shouldn't have, or which category you should or shouldn't expand in. You get to determine what you value most and shape your home around those values. It's a *mindful art* that requires careful decision-making and is deeply personal.

Personally I've lived both extremes of the clutter scale. Growing up I lived as a maximalist. My mom will happily tell you about how much stuff I shoved into my tiny childhood bedroom. Then, when I realized my stuff was weighing me down, I got rid of it. I kept only the bare essentials and tried the whole extreme minimalist backpacking thing. These days, I live happily somewhere in between.

Over the years I've honed in on the categories that bring the most joy to my life and my home. I've said goodbye to categories like DIY supplies, trendy home decor, kitchen gadgets and back stock that take up valuable real estate in my home. Instead, I make space for what I love. So what do I make space for?

My husband and I have a very large book collection that we continually add to. We work from our computers daily, so to us, there's nothing better than coming home to a non-digital book as we sink into the sofa and forget about our day of work. We both love our book collection and I look forward to the day we have a permanent home and a wall of built-in shelves dedicated to showing them off. Do we really need all those books? No, of course not. Does it make us happy? Absolutely. Do we have to make space for it? Definitely.

I also love denim. I love searching for the perfect pair and hunting second hand stores any chance I get. Finding the perfect pair feels like a treasure hunt. It makes me happy, but it does take up space. But that's what's great about Space Making, because by cutting out all of the clutter you get to make space for all those categories that you love. All those things that make you feel something, that make you feel like YOU. Because I cut the useless stuff from my home, I have space to expand on the categories that I do love, like books and denim, and each year I cull through them to continue refining my collections.

In many ways, the true art of being a Space Maker is listening. Why? Because you need to listen closely enough to determine what the clutter is. It's a slow process that takes refining over many years because just as life evolves, so will your priorities for what you make space for. So you keep listening and you keep adjusting.

As you go through **Multiple Passes** of decluttering, strengthening your **Declutter Muscles** and adjusting to living with less, you will get better at listening. Not to the opinions of others, but to yourself. Then you can declare with pride and confidence, "*This is how much I want and need.*"

How to Know You're In the After

It's not an exact science, but there is a very real shift that happens as you move from the **During** to the **After**. It happens in your space, in your mind, in the lightening of your heart and the ease of your breath.

If you're wondering whether you've really made it to the **After**, or if you still need more rounds of decluttering, I want you to read the following statements. Do you agree or disagree with the following statements?

- I am happy with the amount of stuff I have.

- My stuff doesn't make me anxious like it used to.

- I feel like I can breathe easy in my home.

- All the doors in my home can open freely.

- All the drawers in my home can close completely.

- Wow, I'm seriously amazed at how much extra space I have now!

- My *insert room* is not a constant mess.

- I can use my tables and chairs on a daily basis because they are not covered in stuff.

- I don't have any long-term doom rooms or doom piles.

If you find yourself nodding your head and agreeing with most of these statements, then congrats, you've made it to the **After**! However, if these statements don't ring true for you, that's okay! You are probably still in the **During** which means you have more decluttering to do. Stay focused, trust the process, and know that you will reach the **After** on your own time.

If you're on the fence, I suggest you go ahead and move to the **After**. If you still have too many things for your space, that fact will become clear in the organizing phase and we will address it then.

So whether you are a "weak Yes" or a "strong Yes", I say, "Congrats, we're moving forward!"

The After

Introduction to Stage 3: The After

A new beginning is a beautiful thing, and that's exactly what the **After** is. It's a clean slate, a chance to redefine not only how your home looks, but also how it works.

At the beginning of this book I encouraged you to avoid arbitrary rules and instead make your own. Well, now is the time to establish the rules of your household, such as where you store things and how you store them. It's also time to develop guidelines for yourself so that you can maintain your clutter-free space long-term. These are the best kinds of rules and guidelines because they are made by you, for you.

The **After** is when you truly experience the joy that comes not from simply decluttering but from intentionally redesigning your home on your own terms.

In the first chapter, you'll learn how to "Organize Like a Space Maker" by prioritizing function over aesthetics and by always staying aware of the connection between an organized home and an organized mind.

In the second chapter, you'll learn how to "Design Like a Space Maker" by repurposing, rearranging, and using your own treasured items as decor.

And in the final chapter, "The Responsibility is Yours", you will learn that routine maintenance and behavioral change are the two keys to a happily ever after.

Chapter 10
Make Life Easier & More Enjoyable: Organize Like a Space Maker

I'm a self-professed "lazy" organizer because I like to make things as easy as possible. The easier my systems, the more likely it is that my house will stay put together.

The goal of organization should be to make life easier and more enjoyable for everyone in your home.

The strategies I cover in this chapter are designed to make organizing as easy as possible. So let's begin with the two simple actions you will perform as you organize your home.

1. Categorize

2. Contain

Step #1: Categorize Your Belongings According to Their Function

If you were diligent in the During, then you've already done a **Rough Organization** of your home. You were intentional about the things you kept, and as you decluttered you tried to group like items together into broad **Departments**. Now we are going to fine-tune them to fit your needs.

For example, we're going to take your Closet Department and break it down into smaller mini-departments like loungewear, active wear, dresses, and swimsuits. In the kitchen these mini-departments will be things like utensils, glasses, coffee/tea, and spices. In the bathroom you could have haircare, makeup, towels, and cleaning supplies.

Every person will have different groupings according to their needs. As you're refining your **Departments**, ask yourself these two questions:

1. "Does it logically make sense for me to group these items together?"

2. "Will I forget about these items if I put them here?"

You'd be surprised how many illogical groupings I see in my clients' homes. For example, I've seen tortillas and plates organized together. I've seen hot sauce mixed with food coloring. I've even seen underwear stored with baking supplies!

It's easy to lose things when they are grouped illogically. It makes you have to work a lot harder when you are trying to find things around your home.

Make sure you prioritize function over aesthetics as you decide where these **Departments** should be permanently placed. When you approach organizing a particular space, think about how everyone in your home interacts with that space on a daily basis.

For example, if you walk through the door after a long day and naturally drop your coat and bag near the front door, you wouldn't want to organize your space so that you have to walk all the way to the back of the house in order to put away your bag and coat.

Use photos from social media as inspiration, not as copy-and-paste solutions for your home, because pretty won't keep you organized, but functional solutions will.

Step #2: Contain Your Belongings

The way to lock in your **Departments** is to contain them. Give your belongings a very specific home so that they have a place to live. This could mean that you use an actual "container" or that you simply designate an area or zone for that **Department**. Here are just a few examples:

- hanging all winter coats on the same rod and sliding them to the right side of the closet

- putting all the spatulas in the same drawer

- corralling all the kitchen food containers into the same cabinet

- deciding that one end of the kitchen counter will hold all coffee and tea making supplies

- gathering all of your tools into one closet instead of having them spread out in multiple closets

- putting all of the manicure supplies into one basket

- leaving a wooden crate in the entryway for the kids' sporting gear

- designating one shelving unit for decorative dishware and another for office supplies

When you do this, you communicate to yourself and others in your household that *this is where an item should be returned to after use*. "This is officially the electronics, or cutlery, or spices, or gardening department!" You give the home and its occupants a fighting chance to stay organized.

But the real trick of successful organization is to "home" your things in a way that makes sense for your lifestyle. Remember that the goal of organization is to make life easier for the inhabitants of the home; it doesn't need to make sense to outsiders as long as it makes sense for your home's needs.

Experiment With Repurposed Containers

You're not in the **During** anymore, so the **Buy Ban** is lifted! However, this doesn't mean you need to rush to the store and buy all new trays, bins, baskets, and cabinets.

Remember how I told you to set aside and save all of your organizers as you decluttered? If you're anything like my clients, you will have been surprised to realize you had more containers and organizers than you thought.

Because you saved these items, you now have the option to shop what you already own. Even if you don't find a lot of organizers per se, you can get resourceful with what you find. You may find "home decor" items like baskets or decorative bowls that could easily be repurposed as organizing containers. You may have uncovered high-quality boxes like phone or computer boxes that work great for organizing small items in drawers.

This is especially smart when you are first getting organized and testing your systems. You can always upgrade and purchase the "perfect" containers once you've proven to yourself that the system works long-term or after your next pass of decluttering if needed.

Note: My one word of caution is that you shouldn't force a container to work that isn't working.

Take for example my mom. She tried and tried to reuse an old lazy susan she'd had from the 80s in her bathroom. Though she'd been trying to make it work for months, it just wasn't working. Because of this, the space wasn't staying organized.

When I pointed this out to her she realized the same, so we removed the lazy susan and went to the store to find something that would be better. And voila! The new organizer worked like a charm. If the repurposed container doesn't work, at least you tried, but don't force it.

If it's a Pain, Don't Contain

Not everything needs to be placed in a container. Going overboard with containers can have the opposite effect of what we are going for: it can complicate your organization efforts instead of simplifying them.

It can be helpful to contain small items that tend to get lost, but you don't need a drawer or a basket for every single category. Subdividers make sense in some drawers but not all.

There will be times when the best solution is to not use an organizer but simply contain the category by limiting it within a specific area like a drawer, cabinet, shelf or zone within a room.

For example, I love the look of a beautifully organized refrigerator with all of the produce placed in clear organizers. But testing it out in my own fridge made me quickly realize that it was incredibly annoying to maintain. Through this experiment I learned that this type of weekly organizing maintenance (like transferring eggs out of the carton and into clear containers), was not enjoyable. It was an unnecessary chore.

Now I just leave my eggs in their cartons and I don't care how they look. For the rest of the food, I try to zone it off by shelves. It doesn't always stay the most organized but at least it's all contained in one refrigerator behind a closed door.

Laundry soap is another good example of when it can be better not to use an organizer. Detergent is heavy and you may find it easier to simply place it on a designated shelf, labeling the area if you need to so that other members of the household will know where to return it after using.

"Over-containment" can happen when you focus on aesthetics over function. Sometimes you buy a set of matching baskets and feel the need to fill them.

As a rule, "if it's a pain, don't contain."

Clear Containers Make Life Easier

Clear containers are my personal favorite. I think they are the best option for most spaces in most homes.

The reason I love clear containers has to do with what I said earlier: the goal of organizing should be to make life easier and more enjoyable for everyone in your home.

Clear containers make it easy to see what you have at a glance and to quickly find what you need. They make it hard to lose your things or forget that you have them.

The downside to clear containers is that you can see everything inside of them. Especially if you fill them with a lot of smaller items, the container and the space itself might still feel cluttered. Here are two things that I do to counteract this problem.

First, I like to use clear containers when they can be hidden behind closed doors, like in a closet or bathroom cabinet. I don't want to see my clear containers and all of their contents while I am relaxing on the sofa. However, when I do get up and open the door to my office supplies cabinet, I want to quickly glance in my clear containers and easily find what I need, whether it's a pen or a hard drive or a charging cable. These clear containers are keeping me functionally organized while staying hidden from plain sight. As soon as I close the cabinet door, calm is restored.

Secondly, to address the cluttered look that a clear bin can have, I focus on making the very front or the most visible side look calm and organized. Meanwhile, the rest of the bin might be a wild and rebellious mix of things, but that's fine! If you were to open my hallway cabinet today and see the clear bin that I store my extra toiletries in, you would see that it looks calm and organized. You would see an extra deodorant, toothpaste and bar soap all stacked nicely at the end. You might assume that I'm just a crazy organizing lady, but it only appears that way because the end of my bin is so neat and calm. If you pulled out the bin and took a closer look, you'd realize the perfection is an illusion. The inside of the bin is a dump zone for extra toothbrush heads, floss, contact lens cases and lots of other little things.

Maybe it's a lazy approach to organizing, but as long as I can tidy up the front of the bin (or whichever side is most visible), the inside can be the wild west. The most important thing is that it tricks my mind into thinking, "wow, this is a beautiful, calmly organized box."

If you are a perfectionist, this may drive you nuts, but I enjoy organizing this way because it makes me feel less uptight and less like a perfectionist. It's like being a rebel but in the most conservative of ways.

***

Bonus Tip: Budget-Friendly Organizers

Unfortunately, many retailers charge an absurd amount for clear organizers. Some even charge you separately for the lid which I think is absolute robbery. You don't need to pay an arm and a leg for clear containers. There are many affordable options that are similar, if not the exact same, that are just as good and cost a fraction of the price (lids included). If you take care of them, they'll give you years and years of good use.

Go to www.spacemakermethod.com to find a link to my personal favorite clear containers. I settled on these after a ridiculous amount of internet research and trying different brands. They're the ones I use in my home and in all of my clients' homes. I love these particular organizers because they transition well from one space to another. When I move, I simply pack them up and use them in my new place because they transition so well between homes. I like to rotate them around to different areas of my home when I do routine maintenance because they're so adaptable.

Think of Labels as a Form of Communication

Labels communicate where an item's home is so that everyone knows where that item should be returned to. They can be incredibly valuable for ensuring that things stay organized. Of course, at the end of the day the responsibility lies with each person to put things back where they came from.

When I was a kindergarten teacher, I labeled everything in our classroom: glue, scissors, scrap paper, homework books, lunchboxes, etc. All of my students knew where every item in our classroom lived. They knew where to find it and where to return it.

Though it took time for my students to adjust to the habit of returning items to their homes, it eventually became second nature to them. As a bonus, it was less work for me to maintain an orderly classroom. The labels made it so that I no longer needed to remind them throughout the day where things should go. Instead, they were able to take the responsibility upon themselves and learn the discipline of tidiness.

For large families, forgetful partners or shared homes, labels can be a great tool for ensuring your home stays put together. Setting this system in place makes tidying more approachable for even the messiest of people.

Labels can also be beneficial for ensuring things don't get lost. Bathroom shelves are notorious for hiding items in the deep, dark corners, but this is also valuable real-estate and should be used. So that items don't get pushed to the back corners only to be forgotten, I find it helpful to leave obnoxiously long labels so that I don't forget. "Travel Toiletries Bags Are Behind This Basket." Silly, but helpful.

If you don't own a label maker or aren't able to splurge on one, no sweat. Just grab some scrap paper and scotch tape and make your own. It works all the same.

Labels are a form of communication and hold us accountable for putting something back where it came from.

Use the Calming Effect of Closed Storage

The secret to maintaining a calm home while still having real people stuff is closed storage.

Closed storage makes life easy because even if your things are not perfectly organized, you can still close the doors at the end of a long day and experience the effect of a calm and peaceful home.

On the other hand, open storage means more work for you. To keep a calm and orderly home you need to spend more time and effort making things look nice because they are always visible. Even a perfectly clean shelf can appear cluttered if there are too many items stored on top of it.

That being said, if you do have open storage—like a bookshelf, an entertainment console, or anywhere that you are containing things in plain sight—this is one of the few times that I recommend using solid containers instead of clear containers. Clear containers can make these areas feel chaotic and overwhelming even if they are technically doing a good job of containing your items, while solid containers do a better job of calming and bringing order to the space. Baskets and fabric storage boxes are affordable options which come in all shapes and sizes to fit the needs of your space.

When you can, calm your home and mind by hiding your things behind closed storage. While you're relaxing on the sofa at the end of a long day, your things will be out of sight and out of mind.

Mental Space and Inner Peace: The Hidden Superpower of a Space Maker

Do you remember at the beginning of this book when I said, "The state of your home is directly linked to the state of your mind"?

The true essence of organizing like a Space Maker is acknowledging this connection between your home and your mind.

Have you ever felt that you needed to tidy your home before going on vacation? Or that you needed to put away the dishes before settling down to watch a movie? I'm definitely this type of person. Even as a kid I had to organize my room before doing my homework.

I wasn't just procrastinating from doing my homework in those moments (although there might have been a bit of that). I was aware even at a young age that when my space was cluttered, my head was cluttered. I knew that if I could take a moment to organize my space then my brain would follow suit. Afterward, I'd have the mental space to be fully present for whatever task I needed to attend to.

I said earlier that the goal of organization is to make life easy and more enjoyable. But on a deeper level, I want you to realize that as you calm your space you are simultaneously calming your mind.

This is why a Space Maker likes to make organization as simple and easy as possible. Not just so we can avoid doing more work, but also so that we can have clearer minds to attend to the things that really deserve our attention.

This is why the art of Space Making focuses on functional organization instead of magazine-worthy organization. It's why I prefer the ease of closed storage over open storage. And it's why I recommend simple solutions like clear containers with overly descriptive labels on them.

Because when the stress of your unorganized closet/cabinet/pantry is no longer taking up space in your brain, you'll have more time and energy to focus on your family, friends, efforts, hobbies, and endeavors that are truly important.

Chapter 11
Shop Your Own Home: Design Like a Space Maker

What I've learned from my clients is that most of them don't want a trendy, made-for-TV home. Most people want a home that reflects their unique style and tells their story.

Ironically, when I first started helping people in their homes, I set out to help them with interior design. But it didn't take long for me to realize a couple of things.

First of all, I quickly learned that my clients didn't need help with interior design as much as they needed help decluttering. They had nice pieces and good taste, but the root of the problem was too much stuff. I grew more and more passionate about helping them declutter the more I saw how decluttering would change their lives.

Secondly, helping people with interior design was strange because my taste for style never perfectly matched theirs. It was their home, after all. What did it matter what *I* liked? I came to believe that most people already know what they like, even if they don't realize it. And I came to see that my clients didn't need design advice, they simply needed guidance on how to incorporate what they love into their existing interiors, and occasionally some help with the functionality of their space.

The beauty of designing your home like a Space Maker is that you are not starting from scratch! You are not starting in an empty home where you have to go out and buy everything brand new.

You're in a much more exciting situation. You're free of the clutter and your space looks and feels completely new. Now you get to decorate it with *your* decor pieces and *your* cherished memories, which mean so much more to you than store-bought items.

There's nothing wrong with buying some new pieces, but before we shop at the big retailers, we are going to shop your home. We are going to use existing decor, repurposed pieces, and other special items that may have been uncovered in the **During**. This is how we bring life to your space and design a home that tells your story.

In this chapter we'll explore three ways to redesign your home the Space Maker way.

1. Use Your Treasures as Decor

2. Rearrange

3. Repurpose

Use Your Treasures as Decor

Remember how I told you to set aside all of your home decor pieces in the **During**? I told you not to discard them because you never know what you might need or want when you get to the **After** and your home looks completely different.

You worked hard to eliminate the clutter and make space for the things you love. But simply "keeping" those things is not the goal. Especially if you keep them boxed up or out of sight, you are not being mindful of their meaning or their value.

Instead, I want you to bring your cherished items out of their boxes and into the light. I want you to dust them off and display them proudly, to cherish and honor them visually. I want you to see them every day and smile when you think of the people, places, memories, and feelings they evoke. If guests come into your home and inquire about your unique decor, I want you to be able to talk about your life and the things that have meaning to you personally.

This is how you make your home a truly special place, one that can't be copied because it is unique to you and your family and your history.

Instead of looking at clutter, or temporary fashions that anyone could have bought, how much better would it be to look around your space everyday and see pieces that remind you of the best parts of your life?

Don't be afraid to experiment by using heirlooms or special objects as decor. Get creative!

***

Story Time

One of my clients had a bookshelf in her apartment that was absolutely overloaded with stuff. Nothing looked good or stood out on the shelves because all of the clutter blended together.

As we slowly decluttered the bookshelf we kept finding beautiful dishes. The dishes were scattered across different shelves, buried under books and papers and layers of dust. They were very nice and were obviously keepers, so we dusted them off and grouped them together in the most logical place—the dining area.

One day after all the decluttering was done and we were starting to get organized and decorate her space, I suggested that we use all of the dishware to make a display that could serve as the centerpiece of her newly organized dining area. Her eyes lit up with pure joy and enthusiasm. I knew the dishes were beautiful, but I didn't know how meaningful they were to her. It turns out they had all been collected during travels with her mom, and each one represented a precious mother-daughter memory.

Who can say how much those dishes meant to her, or what

> *those memories were worth? Now she would see them every day because they were visible from almost anywhere in the apartment.*

Rearrange Now That You Have Space

In my experience this simple strategy is very underrated. Rearranging your existing furniture and decor can create an incredibly powerful shift in the feel of your space, but most people never even consider it.

Especially if you've lived in your home for a long time, it's easy to think that your current layout is the only option. It's always been that way, right? Maybe you never thought to question why the sofa is on one wall instead of another, or why the bed is shoved into the corner instead of centered.

I'm not just talking about big furniture pieces, either. There's always something that you can move around in your space that will breathe new life into it. And now that the hard work of decluttering is behind you and you have more free space in your home and head, try and take a moment to rethink your current setup.

You might be shocked at how different your space can feel. Sometimes all it takes is a few small changes or swaps. So get creative, grab your measuring tape and get to work!

Ask yourself, "What if I moved the chair over here and the book shelf over here and then made a gallery wall over here? What would that look like?" Or if you're really feeling ambitious you could even brainstorm what it would be like to swap out furniture between different rooms.

***

Story Time

One of my clients wanted to start homeschooling her 7-year-old daughter. However, she and her husband both worked from home and they were desperately short on space. Their apartment had a bedroom, an office, and a third room for their daughter that was completely full of toys and art supplies. There was no room for a bed in the daughter's room so she was sleeping in her parents' bedroom.

My first big suggestion was to completely swap her daughter's room with the office room. The office room was bigger, and I thought the layout could better accommodate her daughter's clothes, toys, art supplies, home school supplies, and even a bed.

This was going to be a huge job because both spaces were full of stuff, but I knew the rearranging would be worth it.

Before the big switch, my client and I did nothing but declutter for 6 days. Each day we filled multiple boxes and trash bags full of papers, office supplies, clothes, toys, art supplies, and

> trash, and piled them by the front door. Her husband would come home in the evening, shocked to see yet another mountain of decluttered items.
>
> In the end we successfully swapped the rooms, and thanks to all the decluttering, the new office room felt bigger even though it was actually smaller. Meanwhile her daughter's new room had plenty of space for her art projects, a desk for homeschooling, and a brand new bed.
>
> A couple years later, my client told me, "Ever since you came to my house, my daughter has been obsessed with interior design, she loves decorating her room and she loves having a space that is hers and only hers."

Repurpose Your Items for a Rewarding Experience

One of my favorite ways to incorporate new design into a home is by repurposing items that are already on hand (usually things that we uncovered in the **During**). These are things like old fabric, dusty shelves, forgotten picture frames, and beat up furniture. I'm always on the lookout for any piece that has the potential to turn into something new.

Whatever you have set aside from your declutter, get creative with how you can reuse it in your home. Could you repaint it? Could you reuse that scrap fabric to reupholster an old chair or to wallpaper your bedroom? There are endless ways to get creative by reusing, repurposing or upcycling what you already have.

Of course, I can't guarantee that your repurposed items will always look better than newly purchased ones. There will be times when they just don't turn out the way you want them to and that's okay. Buying what you need is always an option. But what I can guarantee you is that if you choose to make the most of what you have, those items and projects will bring you a deep sense of pride and satisfaction, far beyond what a store-bought item ever could.

Repurposed items are just one more way to mindfully curate your space and make it uniquely yours.

***

Story Time

I spent the first 18 years of my life growing up in a small city in West Texas that most people haven't heard of it because it's not close to any big city. But if you envision the state of Texas on a map with the word "TEXAS" written across it, I grew up around the letter "E" in a place called San Angelo. I haven't lived in Texas for a long time but although I've lost that Texas twang, I haven't lost the sense of resourcefulness I was raised with.

My parents raised me with the mindset that you should make use of what you have, or even better, improve it if you can. But whatever you do, take good care of the things you own. These ideas play out in different ways across San Angelo, but the main idea is that with a little critical thinking you can solve your problems.

When I wanted to give my friends holiday gifts, but had no money, my parents encouraged me to find creative solutions to my problems. I learned to be resourceful with the materials I had on hand. By using recycled boxes and magazines I found ways to make unique gifts that you couldn't find in stores. I didn't package my holiday or birthday cards in boring white envelopes. My envelopes had colors and magazine clippings and designs all over them—and my friends loved them.

To this day, one of my favorite upcycles I ever did was in one of my college apartments in Portland, Oregon. I wanted to decorate my room but I was broke, so I got creative with an old VHS tape. I took apart the tape, removed the black film and cut strips to create a striped wallpaper pattern on my plain boring walls. From floor to ceiling these stripes extended, secured with staples so they laid flush. And to finish off my design, I used issues of the local newspaper to wallpaper the adjacent wall. It was bold but resourceful. And whenever my roommates had guests over, they always made a detour through my room to show it off, which filled me with immense pride.

I sincerely hope you feel inspired to take your newfound space and make it uniquely yours.

The world of interior design has too much pressure, pretentiousness, and seriousness in my opinion. I want you to take the pressure off of making your home perfect because that was never a realistic goal in the first place. Instead I want you to get creative, have fun, rearrange, upcycle, and boldly display your most treasured possessions.

The clutter used to weigh you down and stifle your plans, but now that you are living with less, you have more freedom to express yourself. Do what's fun for you and your family. Enjoy your **After**!

Chapter 12
Routine Maintenance & Behavioral Change: The Responsibility is Yours

There's no better happily ever after for a Space Maker than the sense of calm that accompanies a clutter-free home. But before you sail off into your happily ever after (AKA, your clutter-free, redesigned, and well-organized home), we need to have one last uncomfortable conversation about this new home that you've worked so hard to create.

I want to be honest about what's required of you so that you never find yourself in that state of chaos again.

Routine Maintenance is the Key to Your Happily Ever After

Unless you're an extreme minimalist with only a toothbrush to your name, your home will require some routine decluttering and organizing. It doesn't mean that you did your declutter wrong or that you are being demoted from your Space Maker title. If anything, it confirms that you are a normal human being (I mean, as normal as any of us are. I'm a little weird around the edges.) We're all busy living our lives, and sometimes our homes lose their rank on our list of priorities.

From time to time your home is going to get chaotic. And when this happens, the best thing you can do is to try and put it back in order before it gets away from you. The more you procrastinate from calming this newly sprouted chaos, the more it compounds with each day. The more it compounds, the less appealing it will be to tackle. If you can stop it before it gets to the point of no return, you'll be saving yourself from lots of unnecessary stress and effort down the road.

To be honest, it's not even important that you have an exact plan for how to perform your routine maintenance. What's more important is that you know that it's coming.

When you became a Space Maker you gained a superpower that makes you more sensitive to clutter. No one can go through the entire Space Maker journey without gaining an appreciation for the work that decluttering takes. You have a 6th sense now. And even better, you have powerful **Declutter Muscles** that you didn't used to have.

You will intuitively know when it's time for routine maintenance because you will feel it. As the clutter slowly creeps into your home, you will grow more and more agitated with the piles. And that's when you'll know that it's time to stop, drop and declutter.

But what's great about having done all of your passes of decluttering is that this routine maintenance won't take you long at all. The hard work is already behind you. This is the fun work of refining all that you keep so that you're surrounded by the things you love.

For many years I would annually go through my home by performing a mini home declutter, but these days that type of thoroughness isn't necessary. Instead, at different times of the year I will quickly declutter any specific piles that may have grown. For me these tend to be work-related piles with papers and material that I may have needed for a project. It's also my junk drawer that seems to attract strings and other miscellaneous cat toys that were hurriedly put away. Or it's my closet.

I especially love my annual clothing declutter because the clothing category is where I tend to make my poorest shopping decisions. Curating my clothes at the beginning of the year is a great reminder of the clothes that I already have in my closet. Each year I get a renewed jolt of inspiration for the pieces that already exist in my wardrobe. It's retail therapy but in the opposite way. Bringing awareness to my wardrobe keeps me shopping less and feeling more inspired to get creative with what I already have. Which brings me to my next point...

Daily, Weekly, Monthly, and Annual Maintenance

If an area of your home is not staying organized, it doesn't necessarily mean that your organizational systems are failing. It could be an indication that you aren't doing the required maintenance.

Change is an inevitable part of life and your organization is ever evolving. You might have a new child or grandchild in the family that alters the things you keep and how you keep them. You might start a new job or pick up a new hobby. The summer ends. The school year begins. All of these changes cause your organizing categories to change or shrink or grow.

Especially when categories grow, it's easy for them to get unorderly. (Think of the coat rack in the winter, or the kitchen cabinets after a grocery shopping haul). Routine maintenance—such as adjusting where and how you store things—is essential to keeping these areas from spiraling out of control.

I like to think of this maintenance on a daily, weekly, monthly, and annual basis.

On a daily basis it is your responsibility to keep things tidy by putting your belongings back where they belong. This responsibility extends to everyone using the space. This is a learned behavior that gets easier over time. If done regularly it will only take a few minutes a day.

Realistically though, our lives can get busy and some days we won't have time to clean up the disorder we've caused. That's normal and it's nothing to feel guilty about. This is where weekly maintenance comes in.

At the end of a long week, it is everyone's responsibility to tidy up and put things back where they belong. For me, my end-of-week maintenance is usually addressing the pile of clothes that accumulated on the floor during the week.

If you didn't have time to clean up after yourself during the week, address it at the week's end. Schedule some time to put everything back where it goes. Set yourself up well for the coming week. If not, the messes will compound.

Monthly and annual maintenance really depend on how much stuff you have. If you're more of a maximalist, you'll need to do more frequent reorganizing. For those with more of a minimalist style, your space will require less maintenance.

For this once-a-month or once-a-year type of maintenance, instead of doing a quick tidy routine, I like to do a full reassessment of what I have. It sounds time consuming, but if you do the proper daily and weekly maintenance, then it's actually quite easy and gets easier the more you do it. Essentially it's a health check on my organizing systems. I'm trying to identify problems so that I can fix them before they get worse. Which areas of my home are trouble spots? Which areas are consistently causing the most frustration? How can I change these areas to work better for my lifestyle?

Routine maintenance on your home doesn't happen by magic. It takes effort. Doing a little bit every day will give your organizing systems the best chance to work.

Experiment with Your Organization Systems

The secret to good organization is to be a good problem solver. You have to be willing to experiment and try things. When something isn't working, you have to reimagine how it might work another way. What exactly is the problem? What are some possible fixes?

If your drawers are getting out of control, the problem may be that your organizers aren't working. Your organizers could be making the drawers difficult to open which means you avoid them. You might just grab what you need and feel less inclined to put it back because you don't want the drawer drama. Maybe the organizers are okay, but you need to allot more space for certain categories so they don't roll over into others. For both of these scenarios, swapping organizers is an obvious solution to your problem.

If your entryway continues to be unorganized and chaotic, take a moment to evaluate the situation. What are the items that keep piling up and how can you create systems for those items that will keep the space more organized? Diagnose the root of the problem and build a solution around *that* so that you can stay more organized in the future.

When I watch organizing shows on TV, they always seem to get the systems right on the first go. This makes for convenient viewing, but it's not how real organizing works in my experience. What really happens is that you get your organizing systems just "okay" on the first round and then you adjust as you go.

If an area isn't working, keep reworking it until it works. Try new things. Get creative. If you give up, your organizing will certainly fail. But as long as you aren't afraid to experiment, you will eventually stumble into an organizing system that works for you. Mastering organization takes time and with more practice you'll get better and better.

Identify and Attend to the Agents of Chaos

Another way to think about routine maintenance is that you are taking the time to identify all of those items that are disrupting your organization. You want to first identify those pesky items and then assign them a home so they don't end up scattered around your house like little agents of chaos.

One thing I see frequently in my clients' homes is they forget to designate an adequate amount of space for recycling and trash related items. Then when they order a delivery meal and don't know where to put the recyclable plastic containers, they just place them on the counter to deal with later.

Chaos breeds chaos. The pile of trash on the counter becomes a trash magnet, making it easier and easier to leave more trash on the counter. Life keeps you busy, and "there's already trash here so there's no harm in adding a little more and dealing with it later." That 'later' tends to get pushed back as the pile grows, making the idea of tackling it less appealing. This is how doom piles are born.

Now that you are a Space Maker you have a higher sensitivity to those out-of-place items. Routine maintenance doesn't just fix problems, it prevents them. This is how you maintain order and a sense of calm in your space for ever after.

***

> ## Bonus Tip: Appreciate How Far You've Come
>
> *Remember the photos you took of your space when you did your **Walk Through**? Now is a good time to revisit these images and reflect on how far you've come.*
>
> *Celebrate your progress! Even if there's still more you want or need to do, take a moment to reflect on where you started. Decluttering is hard work and you deserve to step back and take a moment to revel in your achievements.*
>
> *Your **Before** photos are also a great form of accountability going forward. Reliving these images is often a shocking experience and can be a great reminder that routine maintenance will be necessary in order to keep moving forward and sustain your hard-earned progress.*

Change Your Behavior

There was a sign in my elementary school classroom that I've never forgotten. It was an image of Garfield pointing to his own reflection and it read, "You are responsible for you." The same can be said of your home.

As you've put in the hard work of decluttering, I hope you've started to identify the root causes of your clutter and become more aware of the behaviors that contributed to it. This self-awareness is a crucial step in your Space Making journey, but it's not the final step. There's one incredibly important and potentially uncomfortable step that remains.

Remember the 4th rule of Space Making: Be Open To Change? At the beginning of your journey, I told you that you didn't need to change anything immediately; you merely needed to be open to the idea of change. I asked you to file this idea away for later. Well, later is now.

Being a Space Maker isn't about achieving short-term changes in your home; it's about creating lasting results. To do this, you must not only become aware of the reasons for your clutter but also address and change the behaviors that led to it in the first place. Without this change, your Space Making efforts will be short-lived, and you'll eventually find yourself back where you started.

There are a myriad of behaviors that lead to clutter and it will be up to you to identify those patterns. These are the most common clutter contributing habits that I see in my clients' homes:

- Excessive shopping

- Opening multiples of the same item before finishing the first

- Not returning items to their proper **Departments**

- Buying duplicates too soon

- Ignoring routine maintenance

- Laziness

- Not actively adjusting organization to fit the home

- Bringing home/buying every cute thing you see

Changing these behaviors is not something that can be done overnight; it takes time, practice and discipline. And it's uncomfortable. But as a Space Maker it's not something that we shy away from because to us, the benefits of having a calm home and a clear mind far outweigh the short-lived gratification of these clutter-causing behaviors.

It doesn't mean that you never get to have fun shopping or you can never have a lazy day again. It means that you are aware of your clutter-causing behaviors. You notice the behavior even as you are doing it. And more often than you did in the past, you are able to keep those behaviors in check.

You've experienced the joy of having a calm space and a calm mind. You've felt the satisfaction of coming home to a space you love, full of the things you love. Let these positive feelings be your motivation for moving forward. You're a Space Maker now, embrace the change.

Stay Connected

I like to think of this book as the brains of the Space Maker Method because it explains everything I believe about the decluttering process from start to finish. And if the book is the brains, then the @SpaceMakerMethod YouTube channel is the heart. The YouTube videos *demonstrate* the method by showing real people, real lives being changed, true struggles, true laughter, true tears—that's why it's the "heart" of the Space Maker community.

I encourage you to engage with this amazing community whether you are at the end of your Space Maker journey or the very beginning. Leave a comment and talk to others who are going through the same things you're going through. Get inspired by watching a video of someone who worked and struggled and made it to the other side. Remember that no matter what you're currently going through, you are not alone.

Plus, I've got some really exciting plans for our wonderful community, and the best way for you to stay up-to-date with the latest Space Maker news, videos, products, and offers is to subscribe to @SpaceMakerMethod on YouTube.

I'll see you there!

Acknowledgements

For the past two years I've been obsessing over this book, which I realize sounds a bit extreme but it's really spot on. I've become far too introverted, have successfully grown out my natural gray hair and have created way too many nicknames for my cat. (Is Bunalufugus even a word?) I'm also not proud of the amount of sweets I stress ate while writing this. But I knew that if I could figure out how to put into words exactly what the Space Maker Method is, it could transform so many more homes and lives around the world.

For these past 730 days, I have racked my brain over every single home I've worked in. I've taken on new clients to test ideas and I've studied countless hours of footage from past projects so that I could synthesize exactly how you can replicate what I do for my clients in your own home. Most importantly, I wanted to spend this time ensuring that this book was filled with as many helpful and actionable steps as possible for you.

I hope that after reading this you feel inspired to start Space Making in your own home and that as you stretch your declutter muscles, you grow more and more confident in what you can do. As you begin your journey, your home will slowly begin to change and with it, so will your life. That sounds crazy, I know, but I've seen it happen with my clients time and time again. There is power in Space Making, but don't just take my word for it, try it for yourself. Wink wink.

Before you head out on your Space Making adventure, I want to thank all those who helped turn this book into a reality. For some, writing a book is no big deal, but to me this is a huge deal! This is a dream come true and I only wish I could fully articulate how incredible it feels to have seen this project through. I'm incredibly proud of this book and everything that went into self-publishing, but it was not without the help of so many.

To start, there would be no Space Maker Method without my YouTube subscribers, some who have been supporting me over the last decade across multiple channels. I can't thank you enough for your support all these years. Equally so, there would be no Space Maker Method without my clients. Thank you for having faith in my process even from the early stages. And to the clients who have so vulnerably opened their home up to the channel, on behalf of the entire community, we thank you. Your bravery has inspired so many others to enact change in their own homes.

To my review readers, this book would be far too long and redundant without your help. Thank you for offering your time, energy and valuable feedback so that we could make this book as helpful as possible. On the same note, a special thank you to both my Dad and Father-in-law, who even on their summer vacation, took the time to pour over this book to provide their professional recommendations.

To my family in both Texas and Oregon, I truly don't know how Jackson, Izzy and I would have survived these past two years without your support. Thank you for believing in me and for letting me test the early ideas of the Space Maker Method in your home. I love you all.

To Izzy, who insisted that she sit in my lap through the entirety of writing the first draft, as uncomfortable as it was, I wouldn't have had it any other way. You will always be the original Un-Helpful Helper. And to the friends who checked in on me throughout this writing process, thank you for being patient with me as I spent so much time with my head in this book. I look forward to now having this project finished so that we can enjoy drinks, laughs and more time together.

To my husband, Jackson, who is not only my partner in all life's adventures, but who dedicated this past year to editing this book. And who, dare I say, obsessed over it as much as I did. How can I ever thank you enough for everything that you gave this book? This book was a dream that you infused with life, and I am forever grateful to have you by my side. Thank you for believing in me. I love you and can't wait for life's next adventure together.

And to you, the reader, I wish you calm minds and happy homes going forward. Thank you for going on this journey with me.

I'll see you all on Sundays.

Happy Space Making,

April

Glossary of Terms

After - The 3rd stage of the Space Maker journey. This is the calm after the storm when we consider more thorough organization and design for your home.

Before - The 1st stage of the Space Maker journey. This is when you mentally prepare yourself for what's to come by setting realistic expectations for your home transformation, asking questions to better understand your clutter, and getting clear about your personal motivations for decluttering.

Buy Ban - Step away from the checkout counter! Don't buy anything while you're in the Before and During. Instead, focus on reusing or repurposing items you already have around the house. Your home is going through a transformation and what you buy early on may not work in the end. It's better to wait until the After to make purchases.

Clutter Cause - This is the underlying cause of your clutter. It's often a stressful life event or a pattern of behavior. There can be many different reasons but there is always an underlying cause. Understanding yours will help you have more compassion for yourself and enable you to make lasting change.

Coffee and Clutter - The best way to start a day of decluttering. Grab a cup of coffee (or tea) with a friend and start chatting about your clutter. Snacks are welcome too! It's a great way to lighten the mood and get you ready for a day of decluttering.

Compass Question - A personalized question designed to help you navigate difficult decisions and motivate you as you look toward your bright, new future.

Declutter Muscles - Just like with any other muscles in your body, the more you exercise them, the stronger they become. As you utilize the tips and tools in this book, you will strengthen your own Declutter Muscles and feel more confident, competent, and efficient as you go along.

Declutter Therapy - The acknowledgment that decluttering is an emotional process that requires you to examine your purchasing choices, your sentimental attachments to your belongings, your past behaviors, and your desire for change.

Department(s) - Groupings or categories of like items. In the During your Departments will be temporary and broad. In the After, as you get organized, your Departments will get more specific and become more permanent.

During - The 2nd stage of the Space Maker journey, also known as the Messy Middle. This is when you literally roll up your sleeves and get to work. It's not pretty, but the sweat and tears are always worth it in the end.

Easy Eight - A simple way to begin decluttering is to take a pile of stuff and begin sorting it into these eight, easy-to-identify categories.

1. Obvious Keepers

2. Trash

3. Expired Items

4. Empty Boxes

5. Duplicates

6. This Goes to a Different Room

7. Obvious Unloved Items

8. I Will Never Use That

Find the Floor - One of five easy ways to start decluttering. The goal is to start making progress by focusing on eliminating clutter on the floor first—an underrated but powerful mental boost.

Greatest Impact - One of five easy ways to start decluttering. Decide which room, area, or category would have the greatest immediate impact on your life if you got control of it today.

Hot Spot(s) - A room, item, or area in your home that makes you feel especially anxious or overwhelmed.

Messy Middle - A nickname for the During which acknowledges the fact that things are going to get worse before they get better. You don't usually see this part of the process on TV because it's not pretty, but it's when the real work happens.

Multiple Passes - For most homes, it's wishful thinking to believe you can declutter your home to 100% satisfaction on the first try. It's next to impossible logistically when things are scattered around the home and in corners you've yet to uncover. What's more realistic is that your home will require more than one round of decluttering (AKA another pass), before you feel fully satisfied. Embracing this idea can help you set more realistic expectations and take the pressure off of trying to get things perfect the first time around.

Quick Win - These are projects you can do quickly, whether they are stand-alone tasks or small chunks of a larger project. Because Quick Wins are such powerful confidence and momentum builders, they can be used at any point in your declutter when you need a pick-me-up.

Rough Organization - The idea that you should not be overly focused on organizing while you are in the During. The point of the During is to focus on decluttering, and any organization that you do should be quick, broad, and simple with the main goal of getting back to the task of decluttering.

Shoulding - A funny word that Space Makers use to avoid making guilt-based decisions. It's a reminder that this is your home transformation and no one else's. So never keep or discard something because you "think you should". Instead, try and make decisions based on what you really want and what's best for your home.

Small Space Shuffle - Decluttering in a small home or a small space can be challenging because there's really no place to put anything. You'll need to move things around a lot—sorting destinations, clutter piles, even furniture—as you work your way through the home. It's like a real-life Tetris game. It's obnoxious, but don't get discouraged! This is simply part of the process when you're working in a small space.

Tried and True - One of five easy ways to start decluttering. These are classic and proven places to start that work for most homes.

1. Bathroom

2. Bedroom

3. Closet

4. Entryway

5. Kitchen

6. Hot Spots

Unlock - One of five easy ways to start decluttering. It's a category, room or area that the rest of the house depends on (often a garage or storage area). If you start by decluttering here, the rest of the project gets much easier.

Use it or Lose it Challenge - A technique for dealing with items that have just recently expired or are about to expire (commonly these are pantry or beauty items). Gather them together and place them somewhere that is easily visible so that you will see them everyday. It's a motivational reminder to either use these items or discard them.

Walk Through - A helpful exercise to perform at the very beginning of your Space Maker journey. The goal is to observe your clutter as objectively as possible. Ask questions to better understand your home, why things are the way they are, and what it is you hope to achieve.

www.ingramcontent.com/pod-product-compliance
Lightning Source LLC
Chambersburg PA
CBHW020332010526
44119CB00002B/40